Pressure Game
Basketball

Pressure Game
Basketball

HARRY L. "MIKE" HARKINS

PARKER PUBLISHING COMPANY, INC.
West Nyack, N.Y.

Library of Congress Cataloging in Publication Data

Harkins, Harry L
    Pressure game basketball.

    Includes index.
    1. Basketball coaching. 2. Basketball--Defense.
3. Basketball--Offense. I. Title.
GV885.3.H36   796.32'32   77-17868
ISBN 0-13-699124-6

Dedication

To the future of our family:

Mike Harkins and his wife, Diane,
Patrice Harkins Feeley and her husband, Tom,
James Harkins,
and the two beautiful granddaughters,
    Shellee Ann Harkins
    Jamee Cameron Harkins

Previous books by the author

Seven Championship-Tested Basketball Offenses
Tempo-Control Basketball
Successful Team Techniques in Basketball

What Pressure Offense and Defense Will Do For You

If there is one word that best describes the pressure game, it is "intensity." Although intensity is one of the most often used words in the basketball coach's vocabulary, its meaning is very often over-simplified to refer to such things as "hustle," "play hard," or "give 110%." It is my contention that the term "intensity" implies playing with desire, intelligence, and control. Coach John Wooden probably came closest in expressing how to best utilize intensity when he said he instructed his teams to play with quickness, but not to hurry. By this, I feel he meant that they were taught to operate to their fullest capacities, but within the framework of their own abilities and the team plan that allowed them to work together. *Pressure Game Basketball* provides team and individual pressure game techniques that will permit a team to play both offensively and defensively with poised intensity.

There is much debate about the strengths and weaknesses of different styles of play in basketball. However, the techniques featured in this book give a team an undeniable advantage because:

1. In sports, the actor usually beats the reactor. These concepts allow a team to constantly force the action.

2. All teams must use and face pressure defenses during a given season. Why not give your players the advantage of using the detailed ideas in this book as their basic game plan?

3. These pressure game methods can be used successfully by a team with average-sized personnel. Not every team is blessed with the strong big man.

4. Teams playing this style use more players in game situations. This leads to better team morale, since all the players feel they are a part of the team's success.

5. Physical conditioning is a by-product. Teams that work hard in practice usually have that something extra it takes to win the close games. These pressure game techniques are very demanding.

6. All of these ideas are team-oriented. This teaches a player that a team's lack of individual talent can be overcome by working together as a unit.

7. The apparent enthusiasm of this style has much fan appeal. People enjoy the high scores that are a natural result of these hustling defenses and the fast-breaking approach to basketball.

8. Successful teams usually have alternate plans that they can turn to when things are going poorly. When using these pressure game tactics, a team will have several pressure defenses that permit them to present a new picture to the opposition when needed.

9. A team using these methods never feels out of a game. The players soon realize that playing pressure defense gives their team the ability to score in spurts.

10. By using the techniques described in this book, your players develop the poised intensity discussed earlier by playing that way each night in practice. They acquire a level of motor ability and mental and emotional conditioning that minimizes mistakes in key situations.

This book covers not only pressure defenses—the offensive side of the pressure game, often neglected, is also featured. It is not enough to be able to run your offense versus standard man-to-man and zone defenses. Modern basketball teams are masters at harassment. To win consistently, a team must have offensive pressure game tactics that work against full court presses, three-quarter court presses, and half court presses. These may be zone, man-to-man, combination, or defenses that change on a certain key.

The success of the United States Olympic Team in beating much taller teams by using multiple pressure game defenses has influenced many coaches to adopt their style. The wise coach will be prepared to meet this onslaught by having a defensive pressure game of his own, and offensive plans to combat those of his rivals. The team tactics in this book will allow a team to do just that.

H. L. "Mike" Harkins

Acknowledgments

Special tribute goes to my wife, Grace, for the hours of typing (and her ability to decipher my handwritten manuscript) and for her meticulous efforts on the diagrams.

Grateful appreciation is also expressed to the sources of my basketball knowledge, including:

Russ Estey and Mike Krino, my high school coaches,

Russ Beichly and Red Cochrane, my college coaches,

The players who have played on my teams,

And the publishers of *The Coaching Clinic, Scholastic Coach, Coach and Athlete,* and *Athletic Journal.*

CONTENTS

1

COACHING THE PRESSURE GAME MAN-TO-MAN DEFENSE

THE CONTAIN DEFENSE

The term "contain" may actually be a misnomer for this defense. It is very much a pressure defense. However, it seeks at all times to prevent the offense from penetrating either by a pass or by a dribble. In this sense, the term "contain" applies.

DEFENSIVE MAN ON THE BALL

The defensive man on the ball no longer has the passive job of staying between his man and the basket. Rather, his job is to harass the man with the ball into making a move that disrupts the opposition's team plan. To do this, he must first assume a functional defensive stance which includes:

1. A staggered stance.
2. His back being straight but with a forward bent plane.
3. His eyes glued on his opponent's belt buckle
4. One hand higher than the ball.
5. His hips down low.
6. His feet shoulder-width apart.
7. His lower hand with the palm facing up.
8. His weight well distributed on both feet with a slight preference to the back foot.
9. His being close enough to touch his opponent.
10. Overplaying his man slightly to his weakside or in a pre-determined direction.

It also must be stressed at all times that defense is played with the feet. The two preferred methods of defensive locomotion are:

1. Step and slide, where the defender steps in the desired direction and slides the trailing foot. This method has the advantage of keeping the defender low and, as a result, provides better balance.

2. The step-step method, which may be the quicker of the two. Whichever is used, the primary defensive move of this defense when you are on the ball is to attack, retreat when the offensive man makes a move toward the basket, and then move laterally to prevent penetration. Above all, the defender must be active and aggressive and know that his teammates are prepared to help him if he gets out of position. Some other tips for the man on the ball are:

1. If your man passes and leaves the play situation area (clears out), don't follow him past the far foul lane line. Nevertheless, you must be prepared to get back to him if he is to receive a pass. (See X1 in Diagram 1-1.)
2. When your man picks up his dribble, tighten up, grow tall, and make him lob over your outstretched arms.

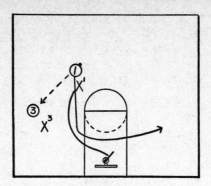

Diagram 1-1

3. If you use your arms too much on defense, it is difficult to move your feet.

4. If your man breaks free for an easy lay-up shot, do not permit him to shoot it. Foul him firmly, but not flagrantly.

5. Don't leave your feet to block a shot except when in the lane, and if you block it, try to keep it on the court.

6. When a shot is taken, you should:

   a. Go directly for the rebound.

   b. Check your man and then go to rebound.

   c. Check and stay with your man. (According to your match-up and/or game plan.)

7. If you must block a shot, do it with your inside (nearest to your opponent) arm.

8. If your man shoots, put a hand in his face

TEAM PRESSURE AND HELP

Versus the two man front

When playing defense against a team utilizing two guards, the following pressure and help assignments are made:

GUARDING THE POST MAN

This defense uses a rotating four man defensive perimeter. This includes the two defensive guards and two forwards. The defensive pivot man is not in the rotation. His job is to man-handle the offensive post man, fronting him except when he sets up foul-line high. At that time, he plays him a strong ¾ and straddles the offensive post man's ballside leg. The defender's arm nearest the ball is up with the hand blocking the vision of the potential pass receiver. When the offensive pivot man slides across the lane to receive a pass after the ball has been passed around the horn, the following rule is stressed: If the pivot man slides across the lane and is foul-line high, beat him across and make your move across the lane inside of him. If he is not foul-line high, stay in front of him, but still beat him across the lane.'' When fronting the post man, the defense should:

1. Disallow any pass to him.
2. Expect help on every lob pass.
3. Call for help on an obvious post-feeding situation.
4. Put your elbow on his chest and your foot between his legs. In that way, you can feel where he is going and still watch the ball.
5. Don't let him cut anywhere.
6. Wheel inside and block him out on a shot.

THE ROTATION VERSUS THE DRIBBLE

Any man guarding a dribbler knows that if his man dribbles to the inside, a defensive guard will help by jumping in the path of the man with the ball. (See Diagram 1-2.) If the dribbler goes baseline, the help will come from a defensive forward. (See Diagram 1-3.)

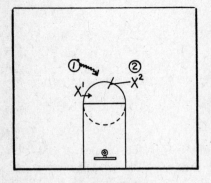

Diagram 1-2

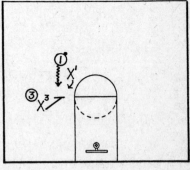

Diagram 1-3

The helper is instructed to jump and help but not to lose sight of his own man. This jump and recover concept has been expanded by some coaches to provide extra pressure on the man with the ball. The players are given the freedom to jump and attack the ball at any time, but they are still required to recover and get back to their man when necessary.

THE BASIC DEFENSIVE PERIMETER

As was pointed out before, this defense against a two man front has a four man rotating defensive perimeter and the defensive post-man handles the offensive post man. As the ball is brought up court, the defensive guard on the ball side pressures the man with the ball. The other three defenders use these two very basic rules:

1. If you are one pass away from the ball, do not allow your man to receive a pass; if you are two or more passes away, you should drop off your man and retreat to the lane. At all times you should be able to see your man and the ball.
2. The offside deep man is the primary helper and the offside front man must help the helper.

The offside deep man or primary helper sloughs off his man and has at least one foot in the lane. He must use split vision and at all times see both his man and the ball. He knows the onside defenders are creating pressure and expecting help from him. He must slide across the lane and stop penetration when:

a. The ball is lobbed to the post man. (See Diagram 1-4.)
b. When the onside forward receives the ball and makes a penetration dribble. (See Diagram 1-5.)
c. On a back door cut by the onside forward. (See Diagram 1-6.)
d. On a screen and roll play and, in general, to stop any penetration. (See Diagram 1-7.)

The offside front man is to drop off and cover the offside deep defender's man on a penetration. (Note: He still must get back to his own man if the ball comes back to that side.)

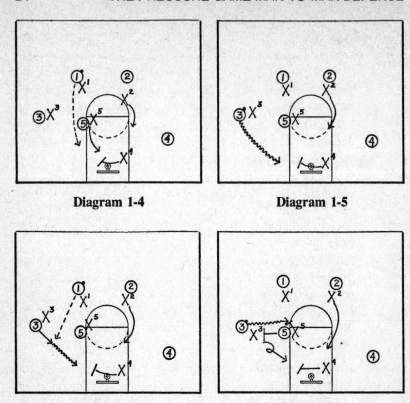

Diagram 1-4   Diagram 1-5

Diagram 1-6   Diagram 1-7

Something that is often overlooked is the importance of preventing the guard-to-guard pass. When this pass is made, the offside deep man becomes a pressure player and must hustle out and overplay his man, and the onside pressure man must loosen up and become the primary helper. These defensive moves are tiring and difficult. (See Diagram 1-8.)

Now that the defensive pressure and help assignments are evident, one can see the dilemma of the guard with the ball. He has four potential receivers:

  1. *The Onside Forward*
     The defender on the onside forward has his head between the ball and his man. His ballside arm is up and his inside

foot is forward. He is determined to prevent the penetration pass to his man and knows he has help from the offside deep man, who is instructed to call out and assure him, "You have help." It also is of value if the onside defensive forward calls for help.

2. *The Post Man*
   The post man is being fronted to an extreme. Again, his defender knows he has help from the offside deep man.

3. *The Offside Guard*
   We have stressed the importance of preventing this pass. It weakens the total defense by changing assignments. It is tough for the defensive guard to stop this pass and still get back to help the primary helper, but defensive guards must have quickness.

4. *The Offside Forward*
   To prevent the offside forward from breaking to the high post and receiving a pass, the offside deep defensive man is told to play as high as his man and to keep an eye on him. In this way, it is easy to beat him to the ball. (See Diagram 1-9.)

Since most teams key their offensive plays with a penetration pass and cut by a guard, we can see how the proper execution of these pressure help principles can disrupt a team's offense.

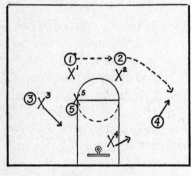

Diagram 1-8

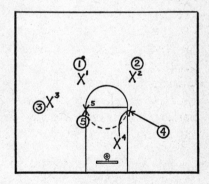

Diagram 1-9

TEAM PRESSURE AND HELP

Versus the one man front

When playing against a team using a one guard front (1-3-1, 1-4, or 1-2-2), the same basic help rules are used in regard to one pass away—pressure; two passes away—help. If done correctly, the offense can really be disrupted because these offenses jam the lane area with people and fail to provide an easy method for the one guard to reverse the ball to the other side of the court. Here are the pressure and help assignments versus the one man front:

THE POINT GUARD DEFENDER

He has three key jobs: 1—As the man with the ball dribbles toward him, he must make it obvious to his team which direction he intends to force the offensive point man. 2—Once he forces him in a given direction, he must not let him out. 3—He should make him pick up his dribble. (See X^1 in Diagram 1-10.)

THE ONSIDE POST MAN'S DEFENDER

Front him and expect help from the offside post man on the lob pass. (See X^4 in Diagram 1-10.)

THE ONSIDE FORWARD'S (WING) DEFENDER

This is the same job as the forward pressure when facing the two man front, but you are sure that a big man is your helper. (See X^2 in Diagram 1-10.)

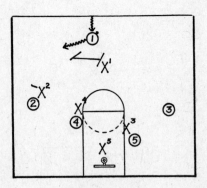

Diagram 1-10

THE OFFSIDE POST

You are the offside deep primary helper. You must protect on penetration moves. (See X^5 in Diagram 1-10.)

THE OFFSIDE FORWARD'S (WING) DEFENDER

You must help the helper. It is a good idea for you to touch the offside post offensive man. Another key job is for you to beat your man to the ball in the event the point man picks up his dribble. (See X^3 in Diagram 1-10.)

TEAM PRESSURE AND HELP

Offensive movement

Once a penetration pass has been made and the offensive players start their cuts, the following rules should be observed:

1. If your man goes away from the basket to screen, you must check the cutter or dribbler and still keep your man. Make the cutter or dribbler go wide and allow your teammate room to slide through. (See X^5 in Diagram 1-11.)

2. If your man is cutting off an offside screen, come over high and beat him to the ball. (See X^2 in Diagram 1-12.)

3. If they have an extreme amount of movement as per shuffle or passing game, anticipate their cuts and draw step-in fouls.

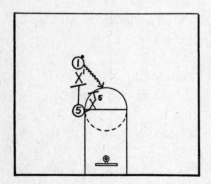

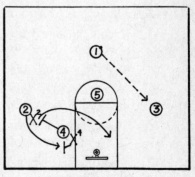

Diagram 1-11   **Diagram 1-12**

4. The screener's man calls the switch.

5. If they split the post, switch, get close to the post man, and force your man to the outside. (See X^1 and X^2 in Diagram 1-13.)

6. If their guards or forwards exchange sides of the court, the defenders should switch. (See Diagram 1-14.)

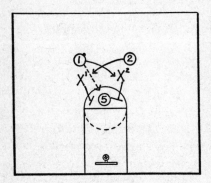
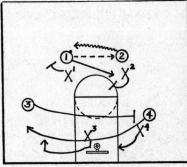

Diagram 1-13   Diagram 1-14

7. Don't clear across the lane.

8. If they work a one-on-one or two-on-two play, where is our help?

9. If our offside deep man beats his man to the ball, they cannot run a backdoor play.

10. If they have a player who overdribbles, double-team him from the blind side.

11. If no switch is called, you must fight over.

12. Our primary goal is to stop the penetration of the ball.

13. If your man sets up in the post, front him and call for help.

14. Know your particular block-out assignment.

15. If you are the offside deep man and your man leaves, tell the offside front man.

16. The defensive man on the ball always has preference. Don't make him go fourth.

17. Talk to your teammates and help them through tight situations by using your hands.

18. Vary the depth at which you meet your man as he comes up to play offense.

19. Know the outside shooting ability of your man. If they have a great pattern, you might have to play very loose on the poor shooters.

20. If they have a five-man moving pattern, be sure to look downcourt after you rebound.

TEAM PRESSURE AND HELP DEFENSIVE DRILLS

Pressure and help

The drill that is most basic to the contain defense is the pressure-and-help drill. It is used to teach the forwards how to prevent the penetration pass on the ballside, and to help on the off side. As shown in Diagram 1-15, the drill is run with two offensive forwards, two defensive forwards, and two guards who act as feeders. In Diagram 1-15, guard (1), is attempting to get the ball in to forward, (3), who is being overplayed by defensive forward, X^3, who is getting offside help from X^4. If (1) cannot get the ball to (3), he reverses the ball to (2), who attempts to pass it to (4), who now is being overplayed by X^4, with X^3 providing the offside help. (See Diagram 1-16.)

The rules of the drill are such that the guards can only pass the ball to the forwards on their side or to the other guard. When the forwards receive the ball, they play one-on-one against their defender. If they beat their defender and penetrate, this causes the helping forward to come across the lane and help. The rule is then

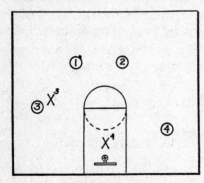
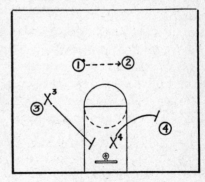

Diagram 1-15   Diagram 1-16

followed by the forward that if someone picks up your man, you must pick up his. (See Diagram 1-17.)

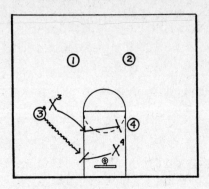

Diagram 1-17

Pressure, help and fast break

The same drill is run, but when the defense obtains the ball, they make an outlet pass to the formerly feeding guard on their side, who dribbles downcourt in the middle lane. The former defensive players fill the two outside lanes, and the former offensive players hustle back on defense. The guard who did not receive the outlet pass drops out. The dribbling guard is not permitted to shoot, but must get the ball to one of the forwards filling the lanes.

One-on-one in the post

In this drill, three passive feeders are used, one at the head of the key and one on each side of the court foul line extended. In the post, X^1 is guarding (1). He is instructed to front the post man and prevent him from scoring. The ball is passed around by the three passive feeders with instructions that most of the feeding should be done by the side men. The defensive help that is needed by a player fronting a post man is provided by the feeding side man away from the ball. He is told to help on the lob pass. This is shown in Diagram 1-18. Side man, (2), has the ball and the offside man, (3), is helping.

When the ball is reversed by way of (4) to (3), (2) is the offside helper and (3) the feeder. (See Diagram 1-19.) If the offensive pivot man, (1), scores, X^1 stays on defense. If not, (1) becomes the defender.

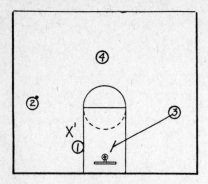

Diagram 1-18

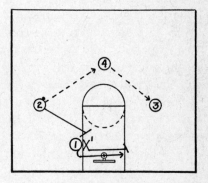

Diagram 1-19

The get over drill

This drill is used to teach defenders to get over a blind screen. The lone defender, X^1, is at the head of the key guarding (1). Offensive screeners, (2) and (3), are stationed at each end of the free throw line in a crouched, hands-on-knees stance. (1) may go in either direction and attempt to run X^1 into one of the screeners. The screeners may not move. The defender, X^1, must flatten out and get over the screen in time to prevent (1) from shooting a lay-up shot. (See Diagram 1-20.) X^1 stays on defense until he is successful.

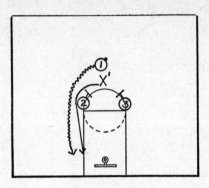

Diagram 1-20

Take the charge drill

The coach stands on the free throw line, facing mid-court. There is a line of players on each side of the court as per a two line lay-up drill. The coach fakes a pass to the first man in one of the lines. This tells him to hustle to the far lay-up slot and take the charge. The ball is then thrown to the first man in the opposite line, who goes hard to the basket for a lay-up shot. The man taking the charge is instructed to face the dribbler in a stance that has his feet shoulders width, knees flexed, and both hands covering his groin area. He then is told to collapse upon contact and take the charge. The coach must point out the inherent dangers of his drill and be sure it is done correctly.

Other defensive drills that should be used are mass slides to stress fundamentals, and break down drills that include the components of some of the basic plays your team will face. Some of these could be splitting the post; screen and roll, guard to guard, and forward to guard; various clearouts; the passing game movement; and handling offside screens.

A checklist should be used by the coach that includes all the defensive components he plans to utilize. An example of such a chart is as follows:

Defensive Check List

Week of: *Eastern Montana College*

DEFENSIVE PHASE	MON.	TUES.	WED.	THURS.	FRI.
1 on 1					
4 on 4					
Slide and Talk					
Stop Shooter					
Over Top Vs. Screen					
Slide Thru Vs. Screen					
Screen & Roll Play					
Clear Out					
Defense on Post (1 on 1)					
The Offside Screen					
Team Rotation on					
Pressure and Help					
Pressure and Help Drill					
Front Cutters					
Ballside and High					
Rebounding					
Gd-Gd Situations					
Gd-Fwd Situations					
Post-Fwd Situations					
Taking the Charge					
Backdoor Play					
Total Minutes					

2

DESIGNING YOUR
ZONE DEFENSE

Coaches who continually make disparaging remarks about zones are usually those who haven't taken the time to learn much about them. If one had to play a single defense for an entire season, it would probably be man-to-man, but there are situations when playing a zone can definitely be an advantage. Some examples are:

— When facing a team that uses a man-to-man offense that does not allow you to capitalize on the strengths of your personnel. This would be exemplified by a very tall, slow, defensive team attempting to cover a quick, patient team running a shuffle or five man passing game.

— To protect a star player who is in foul trouble.

— To change the tempo of a game, and force the opposition to do something other than what they have been very successful with in a given game.

— To protect a lead. Some teams automatically go into a zone when they get an eight or ten point lead.

— To crowd a tall, strong pivot man.

— When the opposition has great one-on-one players, and when they lack teamwork.

— To facilitate your fast break if you intend to run against a particular team.

— In a last-second situation, when the opposition is behind by one, or when the score is tied and they are going for one shot.

— Against a team with poor outside shooters.

Regardless of why you play a zone, you must remember that it bothers many teams. If done correctly, it can be the edge that gives you a victory.

It is very difficult with the proficiency of today's shooters to play a straight even front or odd front zone. The zone game has become a chess match, with the offense attempting to split the seams of the defense, and the defense trying to match the offensive perimeter man on man. This ability to match alleviates the basic problem faced by zones in the past. The zone team formerly was content to give up potential easy perimeter jump shots for the advantage of eliminating the close-in percentage shot. Now it isn't necessary to rob Peter to pay Paul. A strong matching zone can put pressure on the perimeter and still jam the middle. Following are some ideas to consider when designing your zone.

THE INITIAL MATCH-UP

Rotation

The most used match-up method is rotation. This is usually done by starting in an odd front (3-2, 1-2-2, or 1-3-1), and maintaining it if the offense uses an odd front offense. In the event the opposition uses an even front offense, a clockwise rotation is made to match their perimeter. (See Diagram 2-1 and Diagram 2-2.)

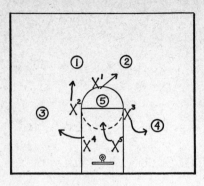

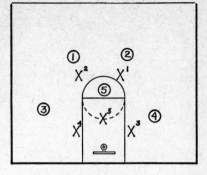

| Diagram 2-1 | Diagram 2-2 |

Monster zone

Another method is to start in an even front zone and maintain it versus even front offenses. In the event the offense plays an odd front offense, one of the guards (X^1, the Monster) drops to the baseline and covers both corners. (See X^1 in Diagram 2-3 and Diagram 2-4.) This converts the zone to a 1-3-1 shape.

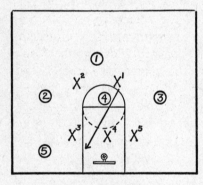

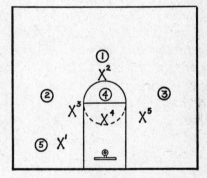

| Diagram 2-3 | Diagram 2-4 |

The middle man adjusting

This is another simple method of matching the offensive perimeter. It necessitates having a very mobile, strong middle man. When the offense plays an odd front, middle man X^1 covers the point man and slides down as the ball is moved toward the corner.

See the front side and corner slides shown in Diagrams 2-5, 2-6, and 2-7.

When the offense plays an even front, the former point man, X^1 drops inside the free throw line and 2-1-2 slides are used. (See Diagram 2-8.)

It should be repeated that X^1 must be both mobile and a strong rebounder.

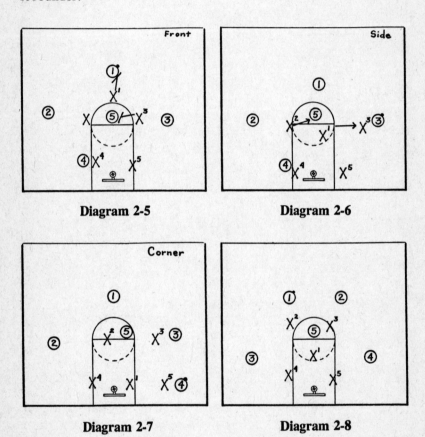

Diagram 2-5   Diagram 2-6

Diagram 2-7   Diagram 2-8

The wheel

Another method of initial match-up is to have a strong re- bounder, X^5, in the middle with instructions to stay between the ball and the basket, and surround him with the other four players. These four men comprise the wheel, and are instructed that they are responsible for covering the next pass (around the perimeter) after the one that was covered by the man on either side of them in the wheel. This might involve changing sides of the court. (See X^4 in Diagram 2-9 and Diagram 2-10.)

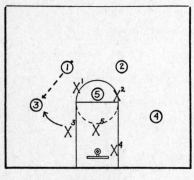

Diagram 2-9

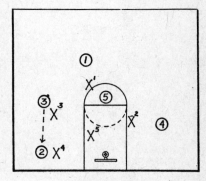

Diagram 2-10

Adjusting by rule

It is possible to give the five defenders rules that complement each other and allow them to cover either an odd or even front zone offense. Starting in a 1-3-1 zone, the rules would be as follows:

X^5 — Stay between the ball and the basket.

X^1 — If there is one man out front, cover him. If there are two men, take the one on the right.

X^2 — Your areas of responsibility in order are (a) up, (b) on, and (c) back.

X^3 — Your areas of responsibility are (a) on and (b) back.

X^4 — If they have a one man front, you cover both corners. If they have a two man front, your rules are (a) on and (b) back on the left side.

(See Diagrams 2-11, 2-12, and 2-13 for the rules in action.)

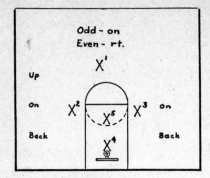

Diagram 2-11

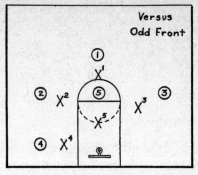

Diagram 2-12

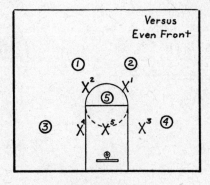

Diagram 2-13

ZONE SLIDES

A team that plans to match the perimeter of their opponents must have zone plans against both odd and even front zone offenses. Following are the 1-2-2 and 2-3 slides used at Eastern Montana College:

Versus odd front offenses

HIGH POST

After the odd front has been matched initially with a 1-2-2 zone, the first consideration is: do they have a high post? If they do, one of the back men of the 1-2-2 moves up and covers him and the zone is converted to a 1-3-1 with the other back man becoming the baseline roamer. It is predetermined which of the two back men will move up with these factors considered. How tall and strong is their high post man? Do they work much to the corner? Do they use a baseline roamer? Do they also have a low post man? The defensive baseline roamer will always play ballside and will cover both corners.

SIDE

When the point man passes the ball to a side, the wing man on that side, X^2, covers, and the two back men slide toward the corner. If there is an offensive man in the corner, the leading man, X^4, goes half way and the trailing back man, X^5, stays eight feet behind him. If there is no offensive man in the corner, the leading big man, X^4, slides on to the lane line and the trailing back man, X^5, stays eight feet behind. (See Diagram 2-14 and Diagram 2-15.)

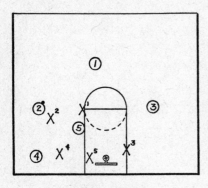

Diagram 2-14

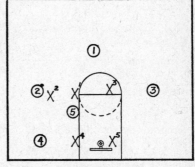

Diagram 2-15

The point man, X^1 always stays between the ball and an imaginary dot in the center of the free throw line. The offside wing man, X^3, has this rule: "When the trailing back man, X^5 in Diagrams 2-14 and 2-15, crosses the lane, you must fill the offside lay-up area. If he does not leave, jam the high post area. You must keep an eye on the trailing back man at all times."

CORNER

When the ball is passed to the corner, it is a moment of decision for the defense.

1. Strong post man

If the offense has a very strong pivot man and low to average outside shooters, a triangle should be made. In this slide, X^2, the man formerly covering the side man, moves down and forms the apex of a triangle, the base of which is formed by the lead back man, X^4, covering the corner and the trailing back man, X^5, eight feet behind him. The apex of this triangle should be about ten feet from the baseline. (See Diagram 2-16 and Diagram 2-17.)

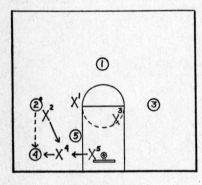
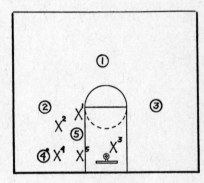

Diagram 2-16   Diagram 2-17

2. Strong shooting perimeter

When the opposition has a very strong outside shooting team, X^2, the man covering the side man (after he passes to the corner) may play between the offensive side man and the man in the corner and disallow the return pass. (See Diagrams 2-18 and 2-19.)

3. Weak ball handlers

When the opposition has weak ball handlers, a corner trap may be run. The defensive side man, X^2, after his man passes to the corner, comes to the ball and along with X^4 double-teams; the point man, X^1, tries to intercept the pass to the side man; and the offside wing, X^3, tries to intercept the lob pass to the ballside offensive front man. (See Diagrams 2-20 and 2-21.) The trailing back man, X^5, is the safety man.

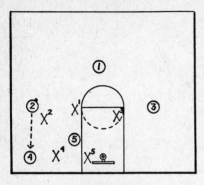

Diagram 2-18

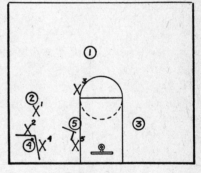

Diagram 2-19

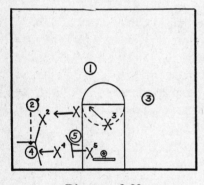

Diagram 2-20

Diagram 2-21

Versus even front offenses

HIGH POST

Although the plan is to use a 2-3 zone, an adjustment is made by X^5 if the opposition has a strong high post man, (5). The middle back man of the 2-3 moves up and plays the high post man 3/4 until the ball is passed to the side. In order for him to do this, both wing men, X^3 and X^4, must start with one foot in the lane and stay there until the ball is passed to a side man. Also, the offside front man, X^2, must jam the high post area. (See Diagram 2-22.)

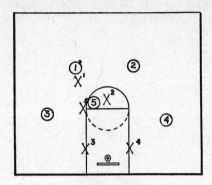

Diagram 2-22

SIDE

As soon as the ball is passed to the side, the middle back man, X^4, resumes his 2-3 slides. From there on, the offside front man must keep the ball out of the high post area in any way he can. He will receive some help from the ballside front man, X^1, who stays between the ball and an imaginary dot in the center of the free throw line. X^3 moves up to take the side man with the ball, and X^4 stays eight feet behind X^5. (See Diagram 2-23.)

CORNER

When the ball is passed to the corner, the same slides may be used as were described previously in this chapter, plus John Egli's innovation of the ballside wing man, X^3, going over the top as shown in Diagram 2-24.

When this method is used, the onside front man, X^1, must cover the next two perimeter passes out of the corner and X^2 must protect for him and be sure no one makes a dribble penetration. (See Diagrams 2-25 and 2-26.)

X^4 has now become the middle back man. If a pass is made to the high post (in spite of X^2), he, X^4, comes up, and X^5 and X^4 must pinch into the lane.

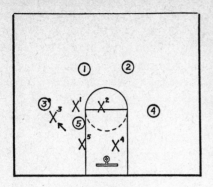

Diagram 2-23

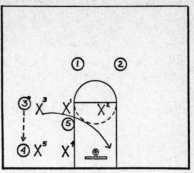

Diagram 2-24

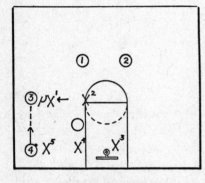

Diagram 2-25

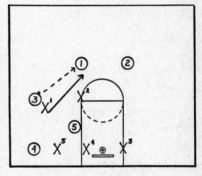

Diagram 2-26

COVERING CUTTERS

Once the initial match-up has been made, and the basic slides determined, the next problem is one of covering cutters through the zone.

Versus an odd front (front man cuts through)

This is usually no problem because the offense must always replace a cutting point man to make sure they maintain defensive balance. Because of this fact, the basic slides will usually suffice.

Versus an odd front (strong side man cuts through)

This cut is usually made after a pass to the corner by the side man. When this play is run, the two wings, X^2 and X^3, and the point man, X^1 may rotate. This is done by the wing man on that side, X^2, going through the cutter; the point man, X^1, coming down to replace him; and the offside wing man, X^3, taking the point position. It is a very good defensive maneuver because the offense usually makes the same rotation to furnish a relief man for the onside cutter, (2). This makes the defense appear to be man-to-man. (See Diagram 2-27 and Diagram 2-28.)

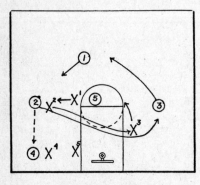
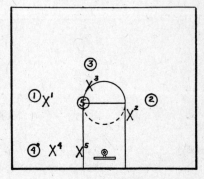

Diagram 2-27   Diagram 2-28

Versus an even front (front man cuts through)

When one of the front men cuts through to the ballside corner, it may be covered in the following ways:

A. MONSTER METHOD

The defender playing the front position on the side of the cutter becomes the Monster. He releases from his front position, calls out "one," and then covers both corners. This converts the 2-3 zone into a 1-3-1. (See Diagrams 2-29 and 2-30.)

B. STRONG OR WEAKSIDE METHOD

The front defender on the side of the cutter, X^2, may go through with the cutter, and if he goes ballside, go with him and play him like a sagging man-to-man defender. (See Diagram 2-31.) In the event the cutter goes to the offside, the defender would return to his original position and sag off if no one is in his area. (See Diagram 2-32.)

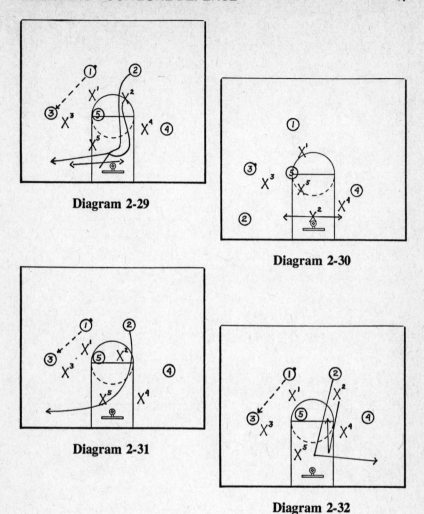

Diagram 2-29

Diagram 2-30

Diagram 2-31

Diagram 2-32

C. OFFSIDE WING COVERS METHOD

When using this method, the offside wing man must cover all cutters. If either a guard (see Diagram 2-33) or a forward (see Diagram 2-34) cuts from the offside, the wing man on that side, X^4, must go with him. He must also alert the defensive guard on his side, X^2, to this fact by calling "cutter."

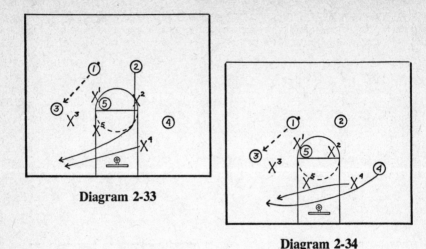

Diagram 2-33

Diagram 2-34

Versus an even front (strong side cutters)

The most often used strong side cut is for a wing man to pass to his corner man, cut through, and then the offense attempts to rotate the ball back around the horn to him. Some methods of covering this play are:

A. CORNER TRAP

This method is to simply run the corner trap that was previously described in this chapter.

B. FRONTING

The next method is to have defender X^3, who had been covering the offensive wing man, slide down and front the offensive post man (5). This permits the defender behind the offensive post man, X^4, to loosen up and cover the man who cut through once the ball is reversed to him. (See Diagrams 2-35, 2-36, and 2-37.)

C. OVER THE TOP

John Egli's "over the top" method has the defensive wing man, X^3, go through with the cutter. All that happens when this is done is that the positions of X^3, X^4, and X^5 are changed, with X^4 now becoming the middle man. (See Diagrams 2-38 and 2-39.)

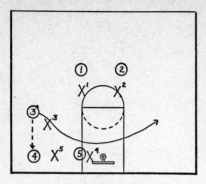

Diagram 2-35

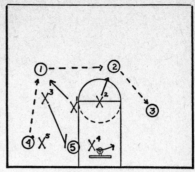

Diagram 2-36

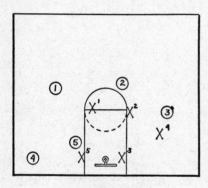

Diagram 2-37

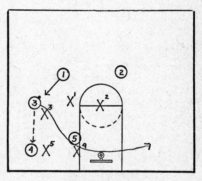

Diagram 2-38

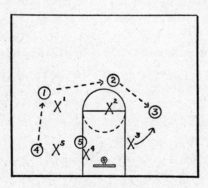

Diagram 2-39

ZONE COACHING ADJUSTMENTS

When designing your zone, you can make slight adjustments in order to give your team an advantage. Examples of this are:

A. Disguising the shape of the zone. This can be done by having your players line up initially in one shape with instructions to use the slides of another. In Diagram 2-40, the defense is in a 1-2-2 shape, but, as soon as the first pass is made, the players utilize 2-3 zone slides as shown in Diagram 2-41.

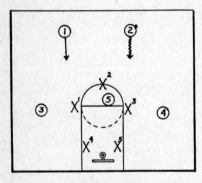
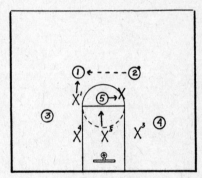

Diagram 2-40   **Diagram 2-41**

In some cases, this simple play will prevent the offensive team from playing in the seams of the zone.

B. Keeping their very strong rebounder in the lane by adjusting their slides. One year Eastern Montana College played Youngstown University, which had a very tall and strong rebounder. They played a 1-2-2 zone, but their big man never covered his corner. The wing man on that side was assigned to cover both the wing and corner on that side. It was the offensive left corner and, since most plays develop to the right, the wing man on that side was very quick; the corner shot is not an easy one and the big man averaged 15 rebounds per game. It was a reasonable gamble.

C. Not worrying about the opposition splitting your zone. Instead, give the zone players this simple rule: "If there is a man in your zone, take him. If he is between the zone areas of you and a teammate, you should double-team him." This rule works especially well from a 1-3-1 zone.

D. Taking advantage of a stereotyped zone offense. Some scouting reports show that the opposition doesn't test one part of your zone. You may adjust your slides accordingly. An example of this would be a team that had a great shooting guard, but never passed the ball to the high post area. This would allow your point man to play up on him and prevent him from getting the ball.

In conclusion, you should be very aware of all the methods of playing against a zone and prepare your team to meet them. These include fast breaking the zone, splitting the seams, overloading, overshifting, cutting through, getting the ball to the high post area, using triangles, throwing cross court passes, screening the slides, pulling the zone out when you are tied or ahead of them, and passing the ball to make the zone work. The zone team must work regularly against these and make specific preparations based on the scouting report for this week's opponent.

3

BLITZING THE OPPOSITION WITH FULL COURT ZONE PRESSURE

Although there are many variations of full court presses, their basic objectives are pretty much the same. The pressing team attempts to:

1. Get into their defensive alignment as quickly as possible (usually after they have scored).
2. Create situations that force the opposition to hurry, make mistakes, and come out of their offensive game plan.
3. Retreat to their basic half court defense after the full court pressure phase of their defensive plan is no longer working to their advantage.

Since these objectives require the ultimate of defensive intensity by the team using them, a well-knit plan is a necessity. Following are two full court zone pressure defenses that may provide the winning edge.

AN ADJUSTING FULL COURT ZONE PRESS

The original shape of this press is 2-2-1. This is based on the assumption that most teams start with two guards, and this changes only when pressure is applied. The two front men, X^1 and X^2, are called chasers; the mid-court duo, X^3 and X^4, are the support men; and the back man, X^5, is the safety man. (See Diagram 3-1.)

This defense is best taught by first giving the players the specific rules of their positions, and then some general rules that they can utilize when confused. The next step is to have them apply these rules to the basic situations they will face.

Specific rules by position

CHASERS (X^1 and X^2)

If the man inbounding the ball is on your side of the court, come up and take him. This will usually be on the offensive right side of the court. You then continue to play a harassing man-to-man on the inbounder until he or the ball reaches the head of the backcourt key.

The chaser who does not guard the inbounder must overplay the man in his area and disallow the pass to him. Don't worry about a lob pass; front him. Stay with him until he or the ball reaches the head of the key.

Don't switch if your man moves parallel to the free throw line.

If your man goes downcourt, don't chase him. Your area ends at the head of the key. Come back and guard the man in your area nearest the ball; jam the middle when the ball is opposite you, and double-team when it comes your way.

The offside chaser should always stay as high as the ball. (See Diagram 3-2.)

When the inbounds pass is received by a man in your area, force him down the side and expect the support man to stop him.

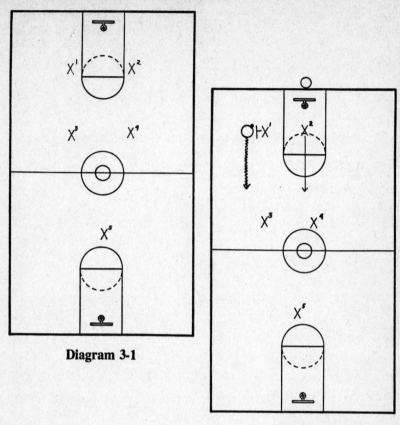

Diagram 3-1

Diagram 3-2

Your job in this double-team will be to seal and disallow the man with the ball from splitting the double-team.

When the press breaks down, beat the ball to the basket.

SUPPORT MEN (X^3 and X^4)

If the chaser on your side of the court takes the inbounds passer and leaves an open man on his side, come up and overplay him and call out "three." This tells the other support man that he must cover the entire mid-court area. (See Diagram 3-3.)

If you have two men in your area, cheat toward the one nearest the ball. (See support man, X^3, in Diagram 3-4.)

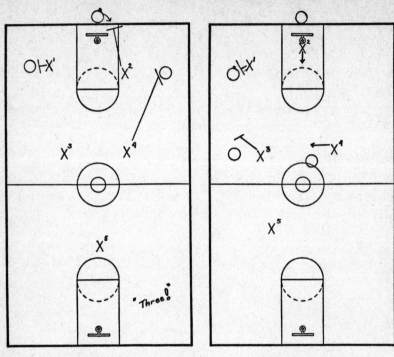

Diagram 3-3   **Diagram 3-4**

If the ball is lobbed over the chaser on your side, you must come up and intercept, draw a foul on the potential receiver, or at least stop him if he receives the ball.

If you are the offside support man and they have a man in the middle, front him. If he breaks up into the chaser area, go with him and call out "three."

If you are the lone support man, move to the ball side.

When the ball is dribbled down the sideline, your job is to stop it. The chaser on the ball will seal.

When the ball goes over your head, on your side of the court, go to the ball and seal the double-team.

When the ball goes over your head and you are on the offside, go to the basket.

If you are the lone support man and the ball goes over your head, run for the basket.

SAFETY MAN (X⁵)

Play as high as you can without allowing a lob pass for a lay-up.

If a pass is thrown from the chaser area to the front court, attempt to intercept.

Once the ball penetrates the support area (past the head of the backcourt key), you retreat and protect the basket.

General rules

This press attempts to start in a zone shape, quickly adjusts to a forcing man-to-man while the ball is in the chaser area, and then to a double-teaming zone press as the ball gets to the support area.

When the ball is in the chaser area, run it down the side.

Stop the penetration of the ball in the support area.

Never run past a potential double-team in the support area.

Once the ball gets to the support area, all five defenders should be on the ball side of the court. (See Diagram 3-5.)

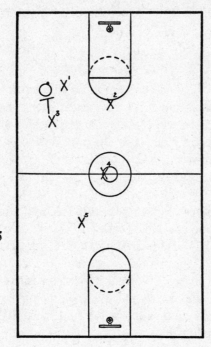

Diagram 3-5

Basic situations

There are four basic situations (assuming the offense is well-organized) which this defense must be prepared to meet.

1. The offense maintains a two man front and the defense is diagnosed as man-to-man.
2. The offense maintains a two man front and the defense is diagnosed a zone.
3. The offense adjusts to a three man front and the defense is diagnosed as man-to-man.
4. The offense adjusts to a three man front and the defense is diagnosed as zone.

(*Note*: The offense's diagnosis of the defense can usually be determined by how much dribbling is done. Teams are taught to pass versus zones and dribble versus man-to-man defenses. Screening and clearing out are also man-to-man techniques.)

SITUATION 1: TWO MAN FRONT VERSUS MAN-TO-MAN

If the offense diagnoses a man-to-man press and still assigns only two men to get the ball inbounds and bring it up-court, it usually means they have guards who are quick and adequate dribblers. First of all, the chaser on the side of the offensive guard attempting to receive the inbounds pass must play between him and the ball and hope he can force a lob pass, which should be anticipated by his support man. (See Diagram 3-6.)

The support man may: (A) intercept, (B) draw a step-in foul, or (C) stop the ball, and the chaser on that side will seal the double-team.

Secondly, once the inbounds pass has been made to the guard, the chaser on that side must be sure he forces him down the side. See Diagram 3-7. He, X^1, must harass the guard enough to prevent him from easily finding an open man in the support area or downcourt. The chaser, X^2, who guarded the inbounds passer must continue to overplay him and disallow a snappy return pass. Any return pass must be a downcourt lob pass, which should be anticipated by the support men in that area.

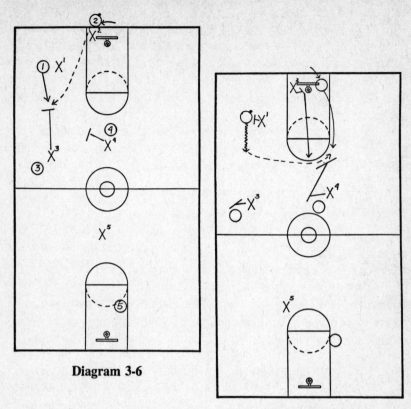

Diagram 3-6

Diagram 3-7

The support man on the ball side must not come up until the
ball is dribbled down the side. At this time, the offside support man,
X^4, must come to the ballside support area and take the man nearest
the ball. If practicable, the support men must make the defense
appear to be man-to-man as long as possible. (*Note:* When the
defense appears to be man-to-man, some teams will invert their
alignment and have the forwards bring the ball upcourt. Since the
chasers are the quickest men, the offense usually is in trouble.)

SITUATION 2: TWO MAN FRONT VERSUS ZONE

When the defense is diagnosed as zone, and the offense maintains a two man front, a lot of responsibility falls on the support

men, X^3 and X^4. The offense will be hesitant about dribbling and will attempt to pass the ball, first to the middle of the court, which is the responsibility of the offside support man, X^4; and, secondly, down the sideline to the area of the ballside support man, X^3. To be safe, the support men, X^3 and X^4, must float in these passing lanes and should not come up to meet the dribbler until they are sure he is out of control. The chaser, X^2, who guarded the inbounds passer will prevent the offense from reversing the ball to the other side of the court by disallowing the return pass. In a zone situation, the safety man must be aware that there is more chance for a long pass.

SITUATION 3: THREE MAN FRONT
VERSUS MAN-TO-MAN

It is my opinion that, when the back court is crowded, the pressing defense has the advantage. The defensive difficulty in this situation is for the support man, on the side of the chaser taking the ball, to spot the open man in the chaser area ahead of him and come up in time. Fortunately, most teams use pre-designated patterns, and the support man on that side shouldn't be slow the second time the offense lines up with what, in effect, are three guards. (See Diagram 3-8.)

It is important that the support man going up to cover the third guard calls out "three." This tells the now lone support man, X^3, he must get to the ballside support area as soon as the ball is inbounded and dribbled down the side. (See Diagram 3-9.) He must also hustle to cover a lob pass over either of the side men, X^1 or X^4. (See Diagram 3-10.)

Once the ball gets to the support area, the defense is in a zone and the idea is to stop the ball and double-team. Note the move of X^4 in Diagram 3-11. Once the ball got past him, he hustled back and sealed the double-team with X^3. Also note that, once the ball gets to the support area, X^1 comes to that side of the court and stays as high as the ball as per zone press practice.

SITUATION 4: THREE MAN FRONT VERSUS ZONE

Most offensive teams keep a safety valve man at mid-court who plays with his back to the basket and helps the guards when

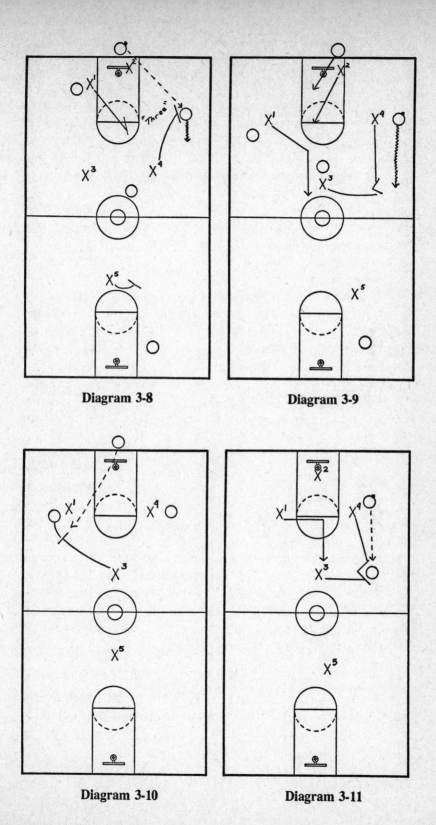

Diagram 3-8

Diagram 3-9

Diagram 3-10

Diagram 3-11

they are in trouble. This is especially true against zone presses. He may stay in the middle or break to the ball side, but if this is true and the offense also has three guards, the back court is crowded and the defense is in an advantageous position.

The big problem area in this situation is how do you cover a cutter into the mid-court area. Here are some tips:

A. The offside of the three defensive front men, X^4, must play almost as high as his man, but sag toward the middle once the ball has gone opposite him. (See Diagram 3-12.)

The lone support man, X^3, must cover the offensive man in his area closest to the ball.

B. The safety man, X^5, must play very high. The fact that the back court is crowded, and the man with the ball is under extreme pressure, allows him to do just this. (See Diagram 3-13.)

Some teams will have three guards and two men at mid-court.

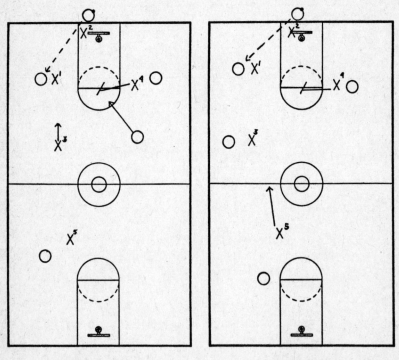

Diagram 3-12   Diagram 3-13

When this happens, the lone support man "deals" with the safety man. That is, the safety man plays almost as high as the support man and the two use this rule: "If the ball comes your way, you are the support man; if it penetrates the support area opposite you, retreat and play the safety position." We call this situation "Five," which refers to the fact that the offense is using five men in the back court. (See Diagram 3-14.)

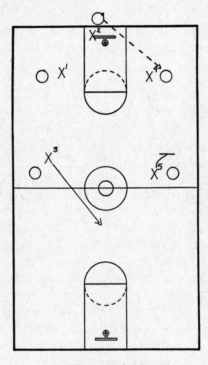

Diagram 3-14

    C. The man guarding the inbounds passer must really hound him and prevent him from spotting an open man at mid-court or in the front court.

    D. Once the inbounds pass has been made to the chaser area, the man with the ball must be played in a manner that forces him to dribble down the side.

    This defense, as with most zone type presses, is best utilized after a made free throw. That way you can assign your players to areas that allow them to quickly get to their defensive assignments.

The adjusting zone press is very difficult to play against, or plan for, because it starts in a zone shape 2-2-1, quickly adjusts to what appears to be a forcing man-to-man, and then becomes a zone press once the ball gets to the support area.

THE 1-2-1-1 FULL COURT ZONE PRESS

One of the distinct advantages of the 1-2-1-1 zone press is that it allows a team to quickly organize their press by using the following methods:

1. Immediately after a score, the team's big, slow player covers the potential inbound passer. This is easy for him because he plays close to the basket on offense.

2. Most teams key their offensive plays by having a guard pass to either the forward on his side, or to the post man, and then cut inside. The other guard ((1) in diagram 3-15) is usually assigned to be the first man back on defense. To utilize this, it is a functional move to assign the guard who cuts inside ((2) in Diagram 3-15) to be the defensive wing man on the offense right side after his team has scored. (See Diagrams 3-15 and 3-16.)

3. The back guard will be the mid-court man once the safety man gets back. His, X^1's rule is to let no one get behind him until the safety man gets back. This leaves the offensive forwards to fill the two remaining zone press positions.

4. This can be done in either of two ways: (A) If the team has one fast forward ((4) in Diagram 3-15), he can become the safety man, and the slower forward (X^3 in Diagram 3-16) becomes the defensive right wing. (B) If the forwards are of equal speed, the offensive forward whose offense position is located in the same floor area as the defensive right wing plays that position. The opposite forward must hustle back to become the safety man.

Once the quick organization rules have been established, this 1-2-1-1 zone press is a rule defense that provides for many double-team situations. The rules are as follows:

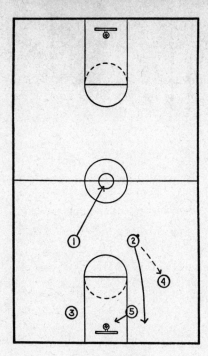

Diagram 3-15

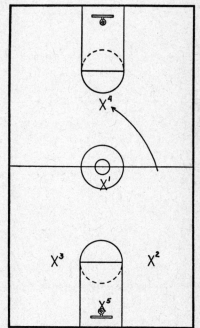

Diagram 3-16

Point man (X⁵ in Diagram 3-17)

1. Bother the inbounds pass.
2. Follow the ball and attempt to seal any double-team that may occur inside the backcourt free throw line.
3. When the ball gets past the free throw line, beat the ball to the basket.

Ballside wing (X² in Diagram 3-17)

1. Stop the ball in front of you.
2. Double-team by sealing when it goes over your head.
3. When you line up initially, move back and to the center of the court if there is no one in front of you.
4. Never let the ball get back to the middle when you stop it. If the dribbler gets by, make him go down the side.
5. The wings cross at mid-court.

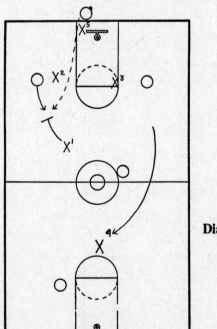

Diagram 3-17

Offside wing (X³ in Diagram 3-17)

1. Cover the middle.
2. Stay as high as the ball at all times.
3. Front the offensive player in the middle of the back court.
4. The wings cross at mid-court.

(*Note*: X²'s and X³'s positions are interchangeable. If the first pass would have come to X³'s side, he would become the onside wing and X² would then be the offside wing.)

Front deep (X¹ in Diagram 3-17)

1. Cheat to the ball side and stop it when it comes toward you. The wing man on that side will seal the double-team.
2. If the ball goes over your head, run for the basket.

Back deep (X⁴ in Diagram 3-17)

1. Play as high as possible without giving up the long pass.
2. When the ball is in back of the far free throw line, intercept any pass that comes into your area.
3. Once the ball gets past the far free throw line, retreat and protect the basket.
4. On any lob pass, you may intercept, try to draw a step-in foul, or just stop the receiver from penetrating.

GENERAL RULES

1. Stop the ball in front of you.
2. Never run past a potential double-team.
3. Always be on the ball side of the court.
4. Beat the ball to the basket.
5. Play defense with your feet. If you must swing at the ball, do so in an upward motion.

The following situations show the rules in action.

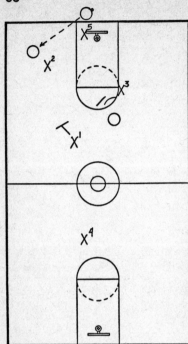

Diagram 3-18.

Pass in.

X^2 stops the ball and X^5, after bothering the inbounds pass, seals the double-team. X^3 fronts the middle man and X_1 comes to the ball side. X^4 plays high and looks for a long pass.

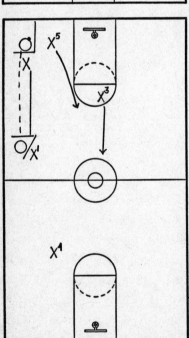

Diagram 3-19.

Pass to mid-court

X^1 stops the ball and X^2 seals. X^5 releases and runs for   sket. X^3 stays in the middle as high as the ball. X^4 plays safe.

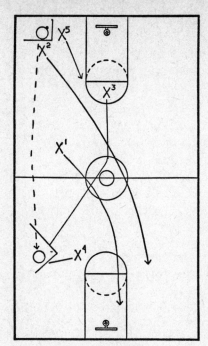

Diagram 3-20.

Long pass.

X^5 releases and runs for the basket. X^3 crosses the court and seals the double-team with X^5. X^4 steals, draws foul, or stops ball. X^1 runs to protect the basket.

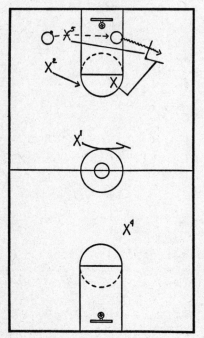

Diagram 3-21.

Cross court pass.

X^5 still attempts to seal the double-team. X^2 and X^3 exchange jobs. X^1 and X^4 hustle to the ball side.

Cross court pass optional methods

Since this particular pass presents a difficult situation for the defense, two other methods of defensing this play may be utilized.

(A) ROTATION

A four man rotation may be made that gives the defense an opportunity to intercept the return pass to the inbounds passer and still not sacrifice its double-team potential. In Diagram 3-22, the inbounder, (1), passes to (2), who is immediately double-teamed by the wing man, X^2, and point man, X^5. The offside wing man, X^3, jams the middle, and front deep man, X^1, swings to the ball side.

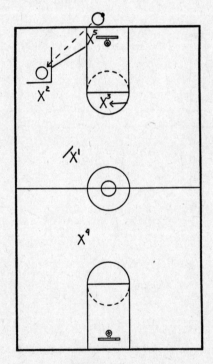

Diagram 3-22

When (1) steps in court and receives the ball back from (2), the rotation begins as offside wing man, X^3, comes up to attempt to intercept or just cover (1). It continues as X^1 rotates to the far wing position, X^2 becomes the front deep man and former point man, X^5 becomes the wing man on the side of the first double-team. (See Diagrams 3-23 and 3-24.) From here, the same double-team opportunities are available.

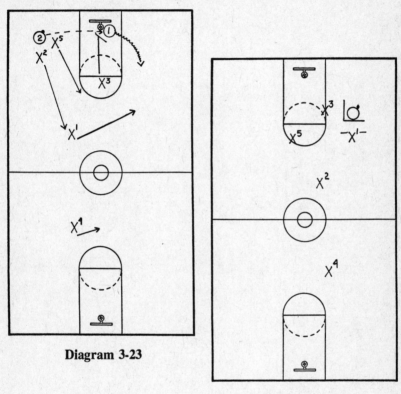

Diagram 3-23

Diagram 3-24

(B) SINGLE OFFSIDE DOUBLE-TEAM

This method ignores the second front double-team once the ball comes back to the inbounder. The only double-team attempted comes after the ball is returned to the inbounder, (1). Wing man X^3 overplays him and forces him down the side, where he is stopped by front deep man, X^1. (See Diagrams 3-25 and 3-26.)

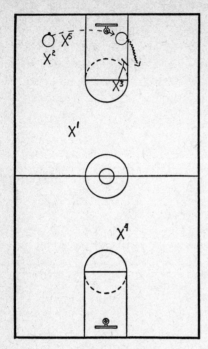

Diagram 3-25

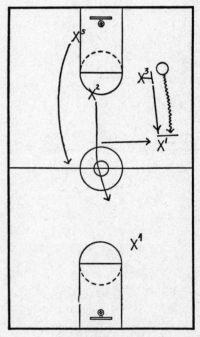

Diagram 3-26

Two-up game

At times, X^4 and X^1 will both play at mid-court until the initial pass in. After that, the one on the ball side becomes the front deep and the other, the back deep. (See Diagram 3-27.)

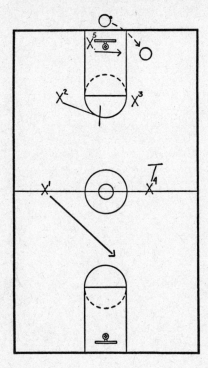

Diagram 3-27.

Two-up Game.

Since the ball was passed to X^4s side, he comes up and X^1 retreats. When this method is used, X^5 must never permit a long pass.

4

CHANGING, COMBINATION, AND DISGUISED DEFENSES

Offensive players have become so skilled at their individual team techniques that, if given the opportunity to "do their thing," they are practically unstoppable. To keep them off balance and unable to establish a rhythm, it is very functional to change defenses frequently or to disguise the defense you are in.

THE FLEXIBLE ZONE PLUS ONE (REVISED)

In 1970 I wrote a book entitled *Tempo Control Basketball*, in which I presented the concept of a flexible zone plus one. Since that time, I have read John Egli's text, *Sliding Zone Defenses*. I now feel the same concept could be used with greater success by using his slides.

The basic idea was to use a four man zone and play their very strong post player man-to-man. Many teams attempt to do this, but without success, because they use either a box-and-one or a diamond-and-one. As a result, it is easy for the opposition to place their players in positions that split the defense and confuse the defenders. Against a box-and-one, the offense can use a one man front as shown in Diagram 4-1.

(*Note:* When the post man (5) plays higher than halfway to the free throw line, the post defender, X^5, plays him ball-side. When (5) moves to the low post position, X^5 should front him.) Against a diamond-and-one, a two man front may be utilized. (See Diagram 4-2.) To counteract this, the coach using the flexible zone plus one concept simply instructs his team to start in a box and, if the opposition plays a two man (even) front, stay in it and it would match them. (See Diagram 4-3.) If the offense plays a one man front (odd), one of the front zone defenders (X^1 in Diagram 4-4) would release and cover both corners. This would allow the defense to match the offensive perimeter at all times, and the man-to-man defender to play his man and get plenty of help from the collapsing zone players.

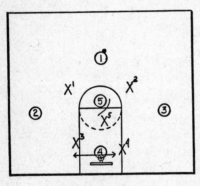

Diagram 4-1

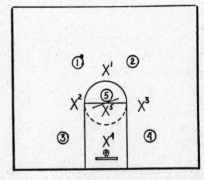

Diagram 4-2

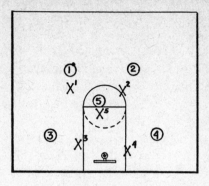

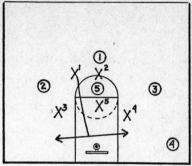

Diagram 4-3   Diagram 4-4

From that point, Coach Egli's zone slides are much better when used with this concept than the ones I presented.

The three pasic zone slide situations are:

EVEN MAN FRONT

Against a two man front, both defensive guards, X^1 and X^2, stay out front and the following slides are used. (See Diagram 4-5.)

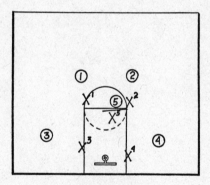

Diagram 4-5

Front

In Diagram 4-5, X^5 is playing (5) (the strong offensive player) man-to-man, and the other four have matched the offensive perimeter.

Front to side

When the ball goes to the side, X^4 comes up and covers it, X^2 and X^1 jam the high post area, X^3 slides across the lane, and X^5 continues to guard (5) man-to-man. (See Diagram 4-6.)

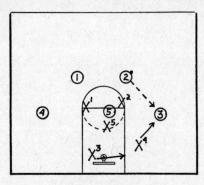

Diagram 4-6

Side to corner

When the ball goes to the corner, X^3 covers it and X^4 goes over the top to X^3's side, X^1 and X^2 jam, and X^5 guards (5) as he comes to the ballside low post area. (See Diagram 4-7.) In the event (5) did not come to the ball, X^4 would slide into the ballside low post area. (See Diagram 4-8.)

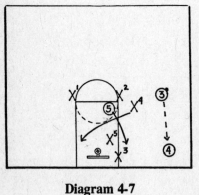

Diagram 4-7

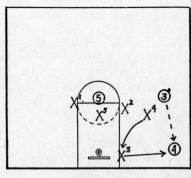

Diagram 4-8

Corner back to side

From here, the front man on the ball side must take the next two passes coming out of the corner. Thus, as the ball goes from corner to side, X^2 covers this pass, X^3 loosens up, X^1 jams from the offside, and X^4 is now the offside wing man. (See Diagram 4-9.)

Side back to front

When the ball goes out front, X^2 takes this second pass out of the corner and the zone is back in its original shape. The only change is that X^3 and X^4 have switched sides. (See Diagram 4-10.)

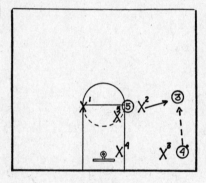

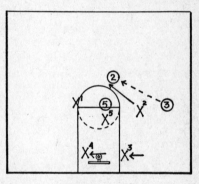

| Diagram 4-9 | Diagram 4-10 |

ODD MAN FRONT

This means the offense is in a one man front, so guard X^1 releases and will cover both corners.

Front

X^2 takes the point and X^1 is now prepared to cover both corners. (See Diagram 4-11.)

Front to side

X^4 takes the pass to the side, X^2 jams the high post, X^1 is prepared to cover the ballside corner, X^3 jams to the offside rebounding area, and X^5 plays (5) in a forcing, overplaying man-to-man. (See Diagram 4-12.)

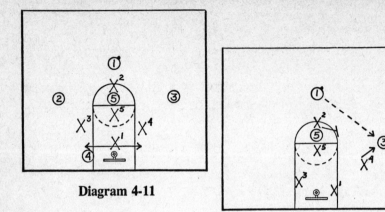

Diagram 4-11

Diagram 4-12

Side to corner

When the ball goes from side to corner, X¹ covers the corner, X³ comes across the lane, X⁴ goes over the top, X² jams in and is prepared to take two passes coming out of the corner, and X⁵ plays (5). (See Diagram 4-13.)

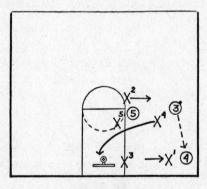

Diagram 4-13

Corner to side to front

X³ and X⁴ have again changed sides, X¹ slides to the ball-side lane, and X² takes both passes. (See Diagrams 4-14 and 4-15.)

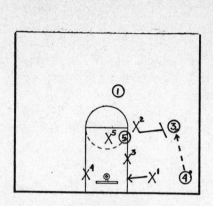

Diagram 4-14

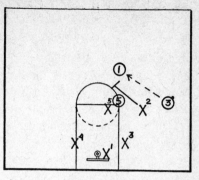

Diagram 4-15

EVEN TO ODD

Many teams start with two guards and cut one through against zones. When this happens, X^1 and X^2 match the two offensive guards and X^1 goes through with the cutter and then covers both corners. (See Diagram 4-16.)

From here, the same slides are used as against odd man fronts.

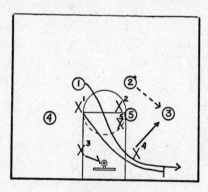

Diagram 4-16

TENNESSEE'S COMBINATION DEFENSE

Probably the greatest exponent of changing and disguised defenses is Ray Mears, the coach at the University of Tennessee. His teams at Tennessee, and before that, at Wittenberg, have always featured defenses that confuse the opposition. They provide constant pressure on the ball as per man-to-man defense, but they also jam the primary scoring area in zone fashion. One of the defenses Mears has featured is what he calls his combination defense.

The object is to get the other team to play their zone offense, which is usually stationary, against your man-to-man defense. Many teams will scout it and, as a result, move against it, but few move fast enough or long enough.

The original set-up is a 1-3-1 zone. (See Diagram 4-17.)

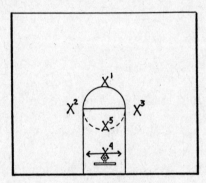

Diagram 4-17

The players must show the zone by their stance and by a symmetric 1-3-1 alignment. From here, the following rules by position are followed:

Point man

1. He must call and point early which man is his. The other defenders key on him and fill in accordingly.
2. If the offense has a two man front, he takes the man away from the team's small wing man of the 1-3-1 zone.
3. He then overplays the man he has chosen, in the direction the game plan has dictated.
4. If, after the first pass, the offense is stationary, he drops to the foul line area between his man and the basket, facing the ball.

5. If, after the first pass, his man moves toward the ball, he must go with him and try to prevent a return pass. He stays with his man until he can safely trade him off. This requires oral communication among the defenders. (See Diagram 4-18.)

6. If his man moves away from the ball, he, (X^1) drops to the foul line area, faces the ball, forgets his original man, and waits for the next man to enter the vacated area. This man is called the release man, and he will always come because most zone offenses occupy the zone areas adjacent to the ball. (See Diagram 4-19.)

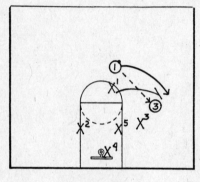

Diagram 4-18

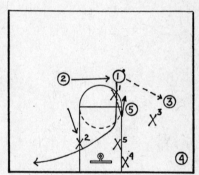

Diagram 4-19

7. When the two front offensive men cross out front, a switch is made, and is called.

8. He, X^1, never double-teams out front, but he may do so on the strong pivot man.

9. When a pass is made to the pivot man inside, he must turn halfway and keep the man in his assigned area in sight.

10. When a shot is taken, he is responsible for the deep rebound to the foul line area.

Wing men

1. Must cover the man closest to the point man on his side. (See X^2 and X^3 in Diagram 4-20 versus an odd front, and Diagram 4-21 versus an even front.)

2. If the man in your area has the ball, overplay him toward the middle. If he is an excellent shooter, force him to the corner and you will get help on him.

3. *Offense Stationary*

   If the pass goes away from the man in your area, collapse toward the basket, between your man and the basket but facing the ball. Play just deep enough to be able to recover on a return pass. If there is trouble underneath, gamble and, if necessary, give the man in your area the outside shot. (See X^2 in Diagram 4-22 and Diagram 4-23.)

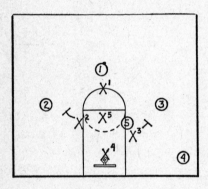

Diagram 4-20

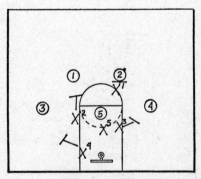

Diagram 4-21

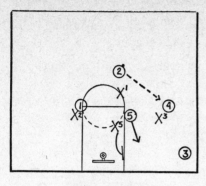

Diagram 4-22

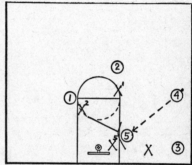

Diagram 4-23

4. *Offense Moving*

   If your man cuts through the pivot area and:

   A. The opposition has a weak or small pivot man, switch off with your defensive pivot man.

   B. The opposition has a very strong big man, go with your man (slide through).

   C. If he goes toward a heavily congested area, let him go. One zone player can cover two offensive men in an overloaded area.

5. When the ball goes away from you and they overload, you are the back man and can see the whole floor. You must talk and direct the defense from the rear.

6. You can double-team in the pivot area or corner, but not out front.

7. If the player in your area is a great shooter, shut off the passing lane. You cannot collapse as far as you normally

would when the ball goes away from you. (See X^2 in Diagram 4-24.)

8. Block out on a shot and enable our big man to get the ball.

9. When the ball goes to the opposite corner and you are under, play high enough to keep it in sight, and when a shot is taken, beat the opposition to good position underneath. (See X^2 in Diagram 4-25.)

10. If the ball is away from you and their post man comes out, switch with your defensive pivot man. (See X^2 in Diagram 4-26.)

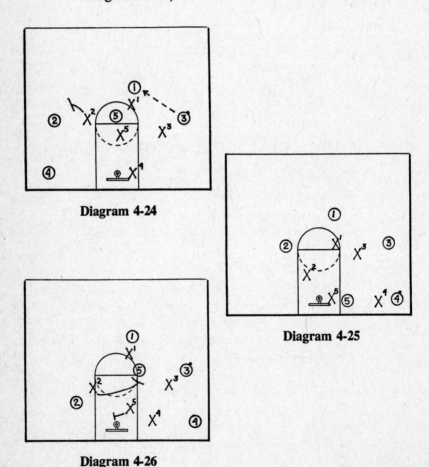

Diagram 4-24

Diagram 4-25

Diagram 4-26

BACK MAN

1. If they have a two man front, you will become a wing man on the small side. (See X^4 in Diagram 4-27.)

2. You help direct the defense and help the pivot man as much as possible.

3. Cover both corners and overplay toward congestion. Don't give the baseline to the player with the ball.

4. Switch with the pivot man when necessary.

5. Block out ballside and beat the corner man to position. You are the second rebounder.

6. Watch the point man to see the direction you will move.

7. Always be on the ball side versus a one man front.

Pivot man

1. You must be the primary rebounder.

2. If they play a 1-2-2 offense, you must cover one corner and X^4 the other. (See Diagram 4-28.)

3. Never let their post man cut cleanly to the ball side. Beat him to the position.

4. If the post man cuts high and receives a pass, you must go with him until help arrives.

5. You can overplay a strong pivot man and violate the rule of staying between the ball and basket.

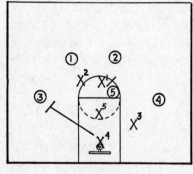

Diagram 4-27

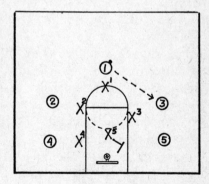

Diagram 4-28

General rules

1. Play between the man in your area and the basket, and as the ball goes away from you, collapse far enough to jam the middle and still be able to get back on a return pass.

2. Face the ball with your hands up to show zone.

3. Talk to help out. Push your teammate to a desired position if necessary.

4. If your man cuts away from the ball when it is on the side, forget him and take the next man who enters your area.

5. Never double-team outside.

6. If your man cuts toward the ball or the scoring area, stay with him until he can be traded off.

7. Do everything possible to keep your big man, X^5, in the lane area. Talk and switch off when possible. At times you may have to cover two men in your area.

Other defensive ideas

CHANGING DEFENSES (Score Zone, No Score, Man-to-Man)

One of the most commonly used methods of changing defenses is to play man-to-man when your team does not score, and zone when you do. It helps a lot if the man-to-man defense being played is a switching type that is easily confused with a zone. The zone should be a matching type that has many of the features of man-to-man defenses. While playing the zone, it adds to the confusion if the defensive players call "switch" on occasion as per the man-to-man defense. It also confuses the offense if the defenders assume a zone type defensive stance (straight up, with hands up) and are in a symmetric 2-3 formation as the offensive team comes upcourt. By the same token, they can "show" man-to-man when playing the zone phase of their defensive plan by assuming a low defensive stance and pointing at their supposed man.

Another variety of this same idea is to play man-to-man when your team does not score, and when you do, zone press and retreat to the zone defense. The point of attack of the zone press can be varied from three-quarters, to full, to a half court press. The point man of the press can key the depth of the press by setting it as high upcourt as he chooses. The other defenders then align themselves with the point man.

Corner change

A defensive change that is very difficult for the offense to adjust to is the corner change. This is done by starting in a zone and staying in it until the ball is passed to a man in either corner. When this is done, the defense changes to man-to-man. (See Diagram 4-29.) This isn't as difficult as one might suppose, because teams that play against zones seldom do much cutting, and it is easy to match up and find a man once the ball gets to the corner. This move, in effect, forces the opposition to start their man-to-man offense from the corner. Few teams are prepared to do this. In the event the offensive team elects to bring the ball back out front and reorganize, it is very easy for the defense to return to their zone. (See Diagram 4-30.)

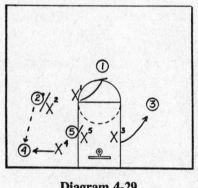

Diagram 4-29

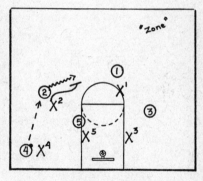

Diagram 4-30

Changing defenses on a number key

Another simple method is to play a "six game." That is, to start in a particular defense, and when the opposition accumulates six points, an automatic defensive change is made. It helps to confuse the offense if the defenders will disguise the new defense. If the change of defenses at six points causes the opposition to call time, a new six game can be organized.

DEFENSIVE HUDDLE

Many teams have adapted the technique of forming a huddle before shooting a free throw. In this huddle, the defensive captain can call any variety of defenses. I feel that this method will soon be disallowed by the rules. Too often the game is delayed by this huddle, and the time allotted for lining up for a free throw was never intended to provide time for team meetings.

A novel variety of signal calling was used by an Eastern Montana College opponent during a recent season. The opposing coach called the defensive signals during free throw break by holding up signs—man-to-man was keyed by a picture of a viking, zone was signaled by a picture of an eagle, and the zone press was called by a picture of a lion.

LEFT SIDE RIGHT SIDE KEYS

A very deceptive defensive change can be accomplished by keying on the first pass and penetration cut made by the offense. The defense assumes an alignment that appears to be a matching zone. Since many teams use two guards, a 2-3 zone will be used as the example. Once the pass has been made to the offensive right side, the defensive guard on that side, X^1, will go through with the cutting guard. This converts the defense to a 1-3-1 shape, and from here a 1-3-1 zone is played. (See Diagram 4-31.)

On the other hand, if the pass and cut are made on the offensive left side, the defensive guard on that side, X^2, still goes through with the cutter, but the defense is man-to-man. (See Diagram 4-32.) Again, it helps if the man-to-man defense is a constantly switching type.

THE ODD OR EVEN SWITCH

A great many teams play a 1-3-1 zone offense. These same teams will play a standard, pro set, man-to-man offense with two guards, two forwards, and a post man. When this situation is

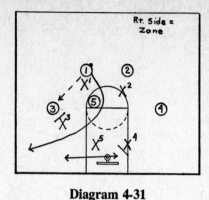

Diagram 4-31

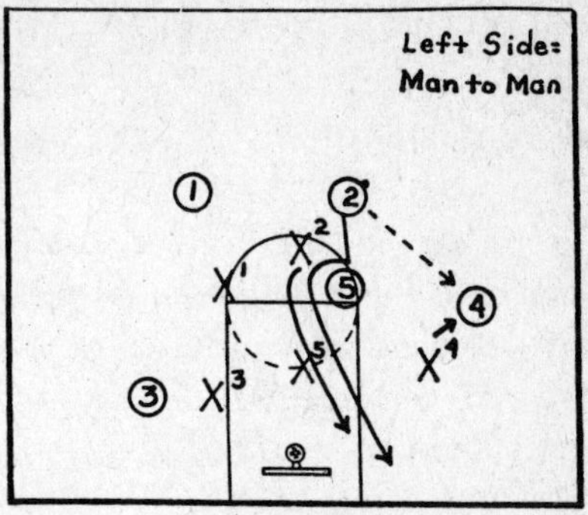

Diagram 4-32

brought to light by a scouting report, the odd or even switch may be made. When the offense lines up in an odd front, the defense is man-to-man. When the offense plays a two man front, the defense is zone.

This defensive plan can backfire if a secondary plan is not developed. During one recent season, Carroll College defeated Eastern Montana College twice during league play by confusing us with this play. During the two week interim between league play and the NAIA Playoff, we changed our offensive plans and ran both our man-to-man and zone offenses from a one man front. The result was that Carroll played man-to-man the entire game and Eastern Montana won a trip to the national tournament.

THE DEFENSIVE FREEZE

When planning your defense against a disciplined pattern team, it might be advantageous to use the defensive freeze. This is a team agreement to play man-to-man for the first three or four passes and then freeze in the lane and convert to a zone. This would work well against teams employing the shuffle, a five man passing game, or the reverse action offense. If the ball is brought out front and an attempt is made to reset into a zone offense, the defense returns to man-to-man for three more passes. This is indicated by calling out "3."

THE CHAMELEON PRESS

After a score, the defense retreats, with the guards stopping at mid-court. From here, the type of press will be called by the direction the guard on the ball forces it. In Diagram 4-33, defensive guard X^1 runs the ball down the side. This keys a double-teaming zone press. If, as shown in Diagram 4-34, X^1 would have run the ball inside to guard X^2, it would have keyed a switching, man-to-man defense or a run-and-jump, non-double-teaming defense.

The defensive guards must be aggressive for this defense to work. Once an offensive guard commits himself to a direction, he must not be allowed to come back.

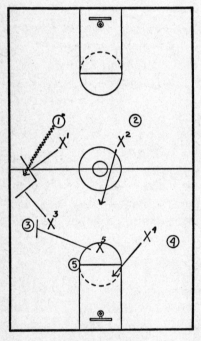

Diagram 4-33

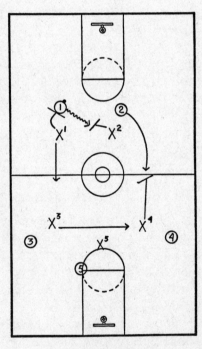

Diagram 4-34

A COMBINATION FULL COURT PRESS

This press consists of three man-to-man defenders, X^1, X^2, and X^3, who dog the opposition's guards (and other men bringing the ball upcourt) from end line to end line. They are aided by a floating zone player at mid-court, X^4, and a zone player playing safety man, X^5.

When the ball is taken out in the back court on the end line, the man throwing it inbounds is ignored. His defender, X^3, double-teams the obvious inbounds receiver. This is usually their key guard. (See Diagram 4-35.) This same formation prevails when the ball is taken out in the back court on the side. (See Diagram 4-36.)

Mid-court man, X^4, plays on the same side of the court as their mid-court man (if any). The safety man, X^5, plays as high as the opposition's deepest player. If the opposition plays two at mid-

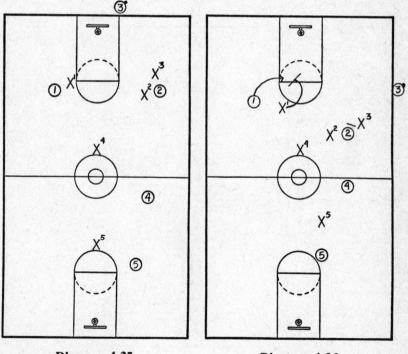

Diagram 4-35   Diagram 4-36

court, X⁴ and X⁵ deal with these rules: "If the ball comes your way, you are the mid-court man. If it goes opposite you, you are the safety man."

Much work is done on preventing the initial pass inbounds. The defenders must not allow the ball to come in, in front of them. Lob passes are covered by the mid-court man, who is instructed to intercept, draw a foul, and at least stop penetration. The time to organize this defense is provided by the coach. He substitutes on every one of his team's violations and made free throws. The time it takes for the new defender to enter gives the team more than adequate time to organize.

Once the ball begrudgingly enters the court, the inbounder is then covered by his original man. From here, the three men up front play a very hard-nosed, man-to-man defense. When the occasion arises, X⁴ can double-team. (See Diagram 4-37.)

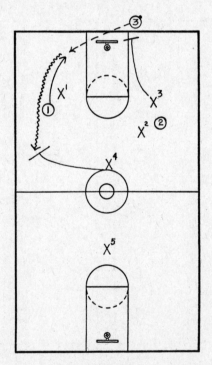

Diagram 4-37

When the ball is taken out in the front court, the inbounds passer is again ignored and his man is placed in a position to help the other four pressure players and to protect the basket. Again, the pass-in is overplayed to an extreme. Diagram 4-38 shows the ball being inbounded from the side and Diagram 4-39 shows it being inbounded from the frontcourt end line.

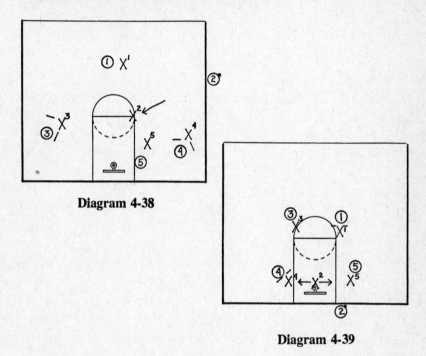

Diagram 4-38

Diagram 4-39

The whole point to this defense is that if you have a floater and overplay the other offensive men to an extreme, it is *very* difficult to get the ball inbounds. Substituting on violations provides time to get organized.

It is also very important for the floating zone players to yell "Ball" once the ball has been inbounded. This permits the defenders to adjust their defensive positions.

Hours must be spent on the inbounds play. The front three defensive players must overcome the fear of the backdoor cut. This defense also permits an alert defender to draw many step-in fouls, because its overplay nature forces much uncontrolled movement.

5

MOVING FOR OFFENSIVE PRESSURE VIA THE THREE MAN PASSING GAME

Until recently, the typical basketball offense was one that could be classified as a static one. The forwards and center went downcourt to their designated positions on the floor and the guards brought the ball up the court. From here, the guards would usually initiate the action by passing to one of the inside men and making a particular cut that keyed a specific set play or continuity. This type of offense was sufficient until the defense, with its overplay and help tactics, began to completely dominate the game. The upsurge in defensive proficiency led to the passing game, which has to be rated as the major force in modern offensive basketball. It began with Robert "Duck" Dowell's (the former Pepperdine College coach) five man passing game, then evolved to the four man passing game plus a post man, and now many teams are examining the three man passing game plus a high-low post.

The big plus factor that the passing game offers over the so-called static offense is freedom of movement. Its advantage over a freelance type game is that the freedom to move is provided, but within the context of a team plan. The governing rules do not chain the players to a certain place on the floor or restrict their individual initiative, but they do allow them some grounds to anticipate the movements of their teammates.

THE THREE MAN PASSING GAME

Although the three man passing game to a certain degree restricts two players to the key area of the floor, it opens up some possibilities that are lacking in either the four or five man games.

The first point that must be emphasized about the three man game is that the two post men may either provide a rebounding advantage over the opposition or, if they fail to do a job, can offer the defense the chance to dominate the boards. This probably underscores a statement made by Jerry Tarkanian, the coach from the University of Nevada at Las Vegas, that the passing game is only as strong as the players who are performing it.

The three man game is a movement-oriented offense which operates on the basis of three sets of rules including:

1. Rules for the three basic movers.
2. Rules for the two post men.
3. General Rules.

It may be used against man-to-man or zone defenses.

Rules for the three basic movers

The basic movers, (1), (2), and (3), are just that. They must move and, in doing so, may utilize each other and the floor positions of the two post men, (4) and (5), in any way they desire. The movers prevent the offense from becoming stereotyped, and thus easier to defense, by using a variety of moves and three man plays, and by playing a number of positions including the point, either wing, or either keep corner. To make their movements functional, they are shown, and drilled on, the potential of the following offensive options:

1. PASS AND PICK OPPOSITE

This is the basic move of the four and five man passing games. It may be initiated by one of the three movers any time he is in the middle of the other two. In Diagram 5-1, point man, (1), passes to wing man, (2), and screens opposite for offside wing man, (3). Wing man, (3), may now: (a) come to the point for a possible jump shot. (See Diagram 5-2.) (b) Use the screen and cut all the way through to the basket, looking for a pass from (2). (See Diagram 5-3.) (c) Go behind the screen when his defensive man prematurely

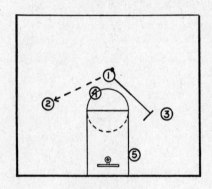

Diagram 5-1

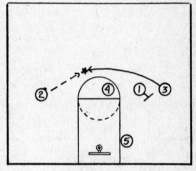

Diagram 5-2

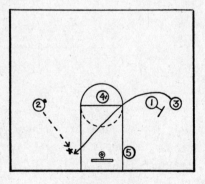

Diagram 5-3

fights over it. This moves plus the positioning of the post men, (4) and (5), in the lane opens up some of the scoring possibilities that are not present in the four and five man passing game offenses. Two examples are:

When player (1) screens opposite for player (3), X^3 fights over the screen, and this tells (3) to go behind, utilize the position of (5) by running X^3 into him, and receive a pass from (2) for a lay-up shot. (See Diagram 5-4.)

Diagram 5-5 shows the offense being run when all three movers, (1), (2), and (3), are on the same side of the court (overbalanced). When player (1) passes to (2) in the corner and screens opposite for (3) at the point, (3) chooses to go behind and utilize high post man, (4), as a natural screen in his cut to the basket.

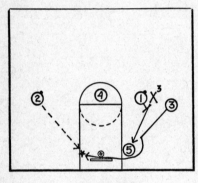

Diagram 5-4

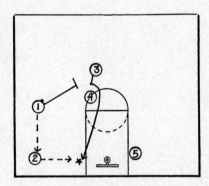

Diagram 5-5

2. PASS AND SCREEN ON THE BALL

Screening on the ball is virtual heresy when running the four and five man passing games, but it is usually incorporated into the three man game. Diagram 5-6 shows movers (1) and (2) using a screen and roll play.

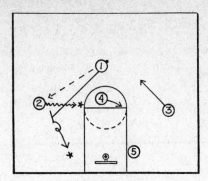

Diagram 5-6

The fact that the low post man, (5), usually plays opposite the ball side gives the screener and the roller room to work.

3. PASS AND CUT THROUGH

In passing game jargon, this is usually called a quick cut. Again, the position of post men, (4) and (5), may be taken advantage of for scoring options. In Diagram 5-7, player (1) passes to (2) and cuts off high post man, (4), for a possible lay-up.

He may have passed to (3) on the opposite wing and cut over (4) for a possible lob pass. (See Diagram 5-8.)

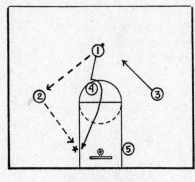

Diagram 5-7

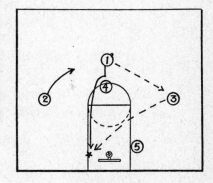

Diagram 5-8

4. LOOP AROUND THE LOW POST MAN

This move, if done correctly, can have the same effect as a stack play. In Diagram 5-9, player (1) passes to wing man, (2), and cuts through. He is replaced at the point by the offside wing man, (3). Player (2) then reverses the ball by way of (3) to (1), who has looped around (5).

In the event X^5 switches, (5) may either be wide open immediately or able to post X^1, who is probably a smaller player.

5. WORK A SPLIT PLAY OFF A POST MAN

This play works best when the offense is overbalanced to one side. In Diagram 5-10, (2) has the ball and passes it to high post man, (4). The three movers then use this rule: "If the pass and screener come my way, we will split the post; if not, I backdoor." In this situation (2) chooses to split the post with point man, (3), and this tells (1) to backdoor out of the corner. In Diagram 5-11, the pass is made to the low post man, (5), from (3), with (2) in his corner and (1) at the point. (3) chooses to split the post with (2), so (1) backdoors and may use (4) to run off his man. (5) looks for a shot or for any of the cutting movers.

6. DRIBBLE OFF A POST MAN

At any time, one of the movers may work a screen and roll play with a post man. Diagram 5-12 shows point man, (1), dribbling off (4) and looking for a shot or for (4) rolling to the basket. Diagram 5-13 shows player (3) dribbling off low post man, (5), with the same two basic options.

7. CLEAR OUT AND MAKE ROOM FOR A ONE-ON-ONE PLAY

In Diagram 5-14, (1) passes to (2) and clears away. This gives (2) room to attempt a one-on-one play.

8. WORK A DRIBBLE CHASE.

In Diagram 5-15, player (1) dribbles at (2) and clears him. (1) then reverses the ball to (2) by way of (3), who has taken the point.

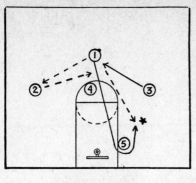

Diagram 5-9

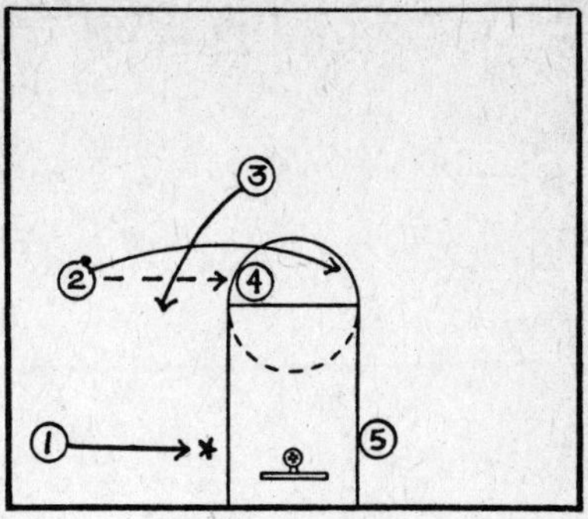

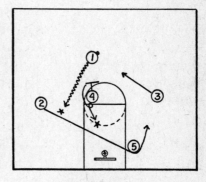

Diagram 5-10

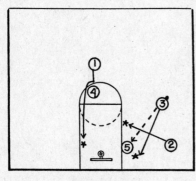

Diagram 5-11

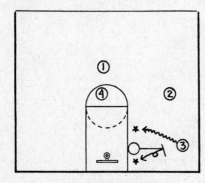

Diagram 5-12

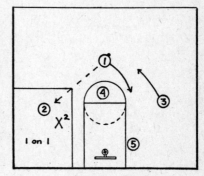

Diagram 5-13

Diagram 5-14

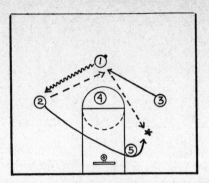

Diagram 5-15

These eight options must be run over and over with no defenses, and broken down into drills until they become second nature. There must be no hesitation. They must be run continually until a good shot can be taken. Once they are run against a live defense, the players will learn to use individual initiatives. The defensive problem is further complicated by the rules given to the post men, which are as follows:

1. If the low post man, (5), breaks high, the high post, (4), must go low. This move often leads to a backdoor play as shown for (3) or (4) in Diagram 5-16.

2. When the high post man, (4), gets the ball, he looks quickly at the movers splitting the post. He then attempts

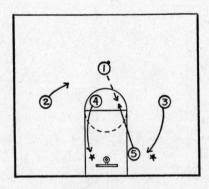

Diagram 5-16

to get the ball into the low post man, (5). (See Diagram 5-17.)

3. High post man, (4), should play very high (to the head of the key) and do a lot of screening.

4. Low post man, (5), should stay opposite the ball 90 percent of the time.

5. Whenever a mover dribbles the ball, the posts exchange. (See Diagram 5-18.)

6. (4) and (5) are the primary rebounders and must storm the boards on every shot.

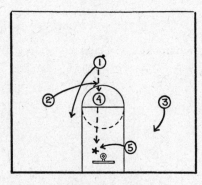

Diagram 5-17

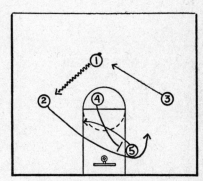

Diagram 5-18

General rules

1. Don't force a shot. Keep moving and a good shot will develop.

2. The post men must get the ball one out of every four or five passes.

3. Don't run the same option twice in a row.

4. The man at the point is responsible for defensive balance. When the play goes away from a wing man, he becomes the new point man.

5. If the initial pass to start the offense is being pressured, the wings may cross and the low post man, (5), may break up. (See Diagram 5-19.)

If no one is open, (1) should use the dribble chase. (See Diagram 5-20.)

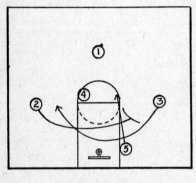

Diagram 5-19

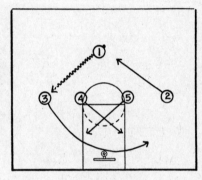

Diagram 5-20

USING THE THREE MAN PASSING GAME
VERSUS ZONE DEFENSES

Some of the three man passing game rules that work well against zones are:

1. Cutting through

When a man cuts through from the point, he may:

(a) Cut to the ball side and create an overload. (See Diagram 5-21.)

(b) Cut opposite the ball and loop around the low post. The ball may then be reversed to him for a jump shot. (See (1) in Diagram 5-22.)

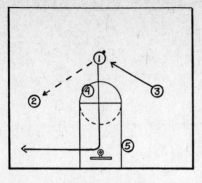

Diagram 5-21

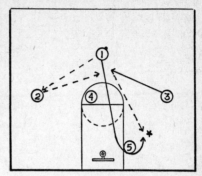

Diagram 5-22

2. Dribble chase

The dribble chase may be used to:

(a) Create an overload. (1) dribbles at wing man, (2), who clears to the ballside corner. (See Diagram 5-23.)

(b) Attempt to catch the defense overshifted. (1) dribbles at wing man, (2), who clears down and loops around (5). The ball is then reversed to him by way of (3). (See Diagram 5-24.)

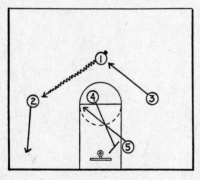

Diagram 5-23

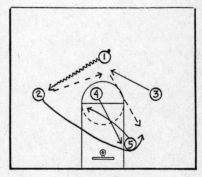

Diagram 5-24

3. Convert the offense to a two man front versus odd front zones

This is done when (1) dribbles toward a sideline and the wing man on that side, (2), clears to the corner. The two man front is accomplished when high post man, (4), steps out on the offside. (See Diagram 5-25.) This move splits the seams of the 1-3-1 zone. (See Diagram 5-26.)

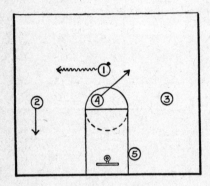

Diagram 5-25

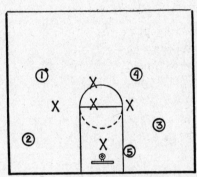

Diagram 5-26

4. Post exchange on dribble key

When one of the movers dribbles such as wing man, (2), in Diagram 5-27, it tells the post men to exchange. Against zone defenses, both post men may stay on the ball side.

When this is done, (4) may be open for a power lay-up or (5), for a jump shot. Very often if the ball is thrown to (5), (4) becomes open. (See Diagram 5-28.)

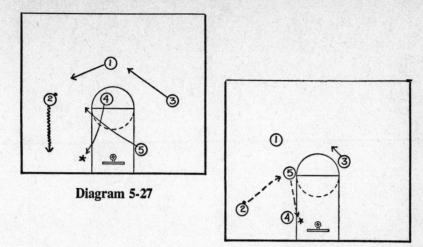

Diagram 5-27

Diagram 5-28

5. Post feeds post

The rule, "when one post gets the ball, he feeds the other," is a very good one against zones. In Diagram 5-29, (5) breaks high, receives the ball, and lobs it to (4) as he goes low.

Finally, it must be stressed that the players must know their roles. Players (4) and (5) must dominate the boards; players (1), (2), and (3) must move and create situations; the point man must maintain defensive balance; and the entire team must be patient, and work for good shots.

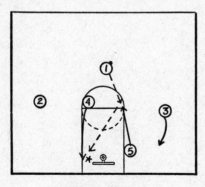

Diagram 5-29

6

BREAKING THE ZONE DEFENSE

During a season, a team can expect to play against zones with various alignments that attempt to match their perimeter, go through with cutters, double-team them, and use various other stunts to make their offensive game difficult. To combat this, a team must have a flexible zone movement that permits them to face any alignment and allows them to adjust to the various zone stunts. The following two zone offenses meet these criteria.

A TWO PHASE FLEXIBLE ZONE OFFENSE

Phase I (box shape)

This phase starts in a box formation with a two guard front, players (1) and (2), two forwards, players (3) and (4), and a high post man, player (5), and has three basic options. It is the ideal alignment with which to face an odd man front (1-2-2, 1-3-1, or 3-2) zone. If the odd front defense does not attempt to make an adjustment that allows it to match the offensive perimeter, the first phase of the continuity is run.

Option 1: In Diagram 6-1, guard (1) starts the movement by passing to his forward, (3), and cutting through the defense and out in the offside corner. The offside guard, (2), replaces him and forward, (4), comes out front to replace (2). The post man, (5), then swings down from the high post to the ballside lay-up area. (3) may now pass to the post man sliding down, or reverse the ball by way of (2) and (4) to (1) in the offside forward slot. As (2) and (4) handle the ball, they must be aware of potential jump shots and, at all times, be offensive minded. (See Diagram 6-1.)

Option 2: The original cutter, (1), also has the option of cutting to the ballside corner. This cut requires the other players to be aware because it delays the rotation movements of the offside players, (2) and (4). Player (3) may now dribble out front to put the offense back in a box formation. (See Diagram 6-2.)

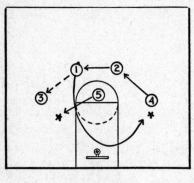

Diagram 6-1

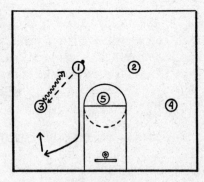

Diagram 6-2

Option 3: Player (3) may pass to (1) in the corner and cut through to the offside. When this happens, (2) must really hustle to get to the ballside guard position to become the release man for (1), who has the ball in the corner. If necessary, (1) may dribble toward (2) if he desires to get the ball to him. (See Diagram 6-3.) Player (4) comes out front, and the offense is back in the box formation against the odd front zone. As the ball is moved around the perimeter, the pivot man, (5), always stays between the ball and a line to the basket.

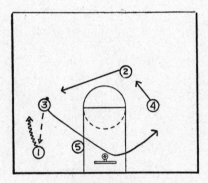

Diagram 6-3

The simple movement created by the offense in these three options permits it to offer enough player movement to force defensive adjustments, and, at the same time, maintains the basic box formation that creates so many problems for the odd front zone.

Phase II (odd front)

This phase is used against even front zones (2-3 and 2-1-2). It starts in the same manner as the box phase with (1) passing to his forward, (3) and cutting through to the offside wing position. The offense is converted to an odd front when the offside forward, (4), cuts to the high post area instead of coming out front. (See (4) in Diagram 6-4.) From here, the player with the ball, (3), may pass to (4) in the middle who, in turn, would look for (5) or (1) in the low post area. (See Diagram 6-5.) Or, (3) may reverse the ball, by way

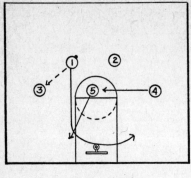

Diagram 6-4

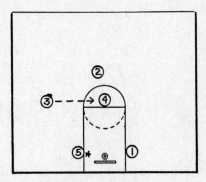

Diagram 6-5

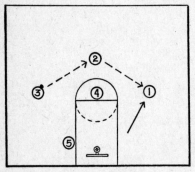

Diagram 6-6

of (2) back to (1) to attempt to catch the defense overshifted. (See Diagram 6-6.)

If the original cutter, (1), cuts to the ballside corner, the following option is run: (1) becomes the baseline roamer, staying always on the ball side, and the offside forward always cuts into the high post area. (See Diagrams 6-7, 6-8, and 6-9.)

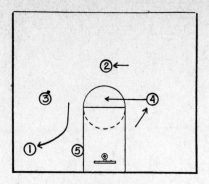

Diagram 6-7

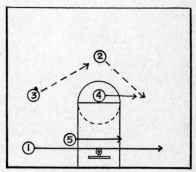

Diagram 6-8

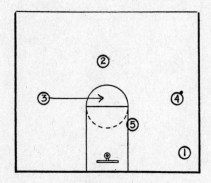

Diagram 6-9

When the ball is passed to (1) in the corner, as shown in Diagram 6-10, the ballside forward, (3), cuts through and is replaced by the offside forward, (4), who has cut to the high post area from the offside. The ball is then reversed around the horn to (3) in an attempt to catch the defense overshifted.

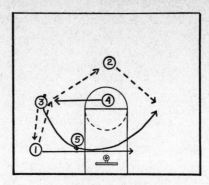

Diagram 6-10

Point dribble special

A special play may be run from this formation with (1) in the corner. After the strongside forward, (3), who is positioned on the same side of the floor as baseline roamer, (1), passes the ball to the point man, (2), (2) dribbles toward the other sideline and fakes a pass to (4) on that side. This shifts the zone to that side and tells (3) to pinch inside and screen for (1), who breaks to the foul line extended and receives a pass from (2) for an unmolested jump shot. (See Diagrams 6-11 and 6-12.)

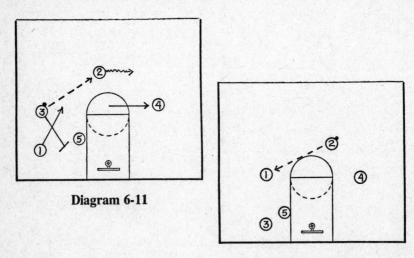

Diagram 6-11

Diagram 6-12

(*Note*: The odd man front offense is maintained as long as the defense plays their even man front zone. When they adjust to an odd front defense, the point man, (2), uses the dribble special to bring (1) back out front and again split the defense. (See Diagrams 6-13 and 6-14.)

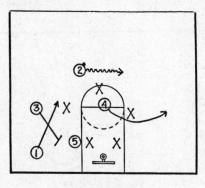

Diagram 6-13

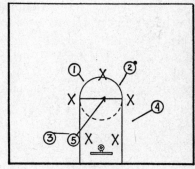

Diagram 6-14

THE 1-3-1 CONTINUITY APPROACH TO FACING ZONES

Probably the most preferred alignment against the zone defense is the 1-3-1. This offense consists of three 1-3-1 continuities, and offers many cuts and screens that are very functional against zones.

THE PASS AND SLASH CONTINUITY

The basic zone play for this offense is a continuity which is keyed when the point man, (1), passes to a wing and slashes off the high post to the offside low post area. This tells the post man, (5), to swing to the ball side, and the offside wing man, (2), to take the point position in order to maintain defensive balance. (See Diagram 6-15.)

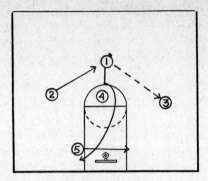

Diagram 6-15

From here, (3) may: (a) pass to (5) for a one-on-one play in the low post area; (b) pass to (4) in the middle of the zone (Note: In this event, players (1) and (5) are very often open for power lay-up shots); or (c) pass the ball out front to (2), who would reverse the ball to (1) as he broke to the wing. In this case, an inside rotation would take place. As (1) received the ball, (4) would slide to the ballside low post area and the offside wing man, (3), would cut to the high post. (See Diagram 6-16.)

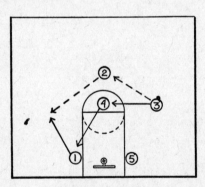

Diagram 6-16

Player (1) would have the same three options. He could hit (4) sliding to the low post, (3) cutting to the high post, or reverse the ball to (5) breaking out to the wing position and cause another inside rotation to occur. (See Diagrams 6-17 and 6-18.)

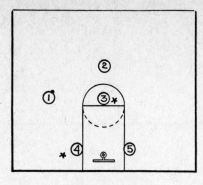

Diagram 6-17

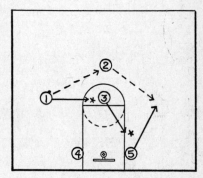

Diagram 6-18

If, during this rotation, the ballside low post man, (3), moves halfway to the corner and receives a pass from the man with the ball, (5), this keys the now high post man, (1), to cut down toward the basket and expect a pass from (3) for a power lay-up. (See Diagram 6-19.)

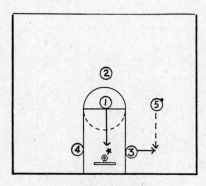

Diagram 6-19

In the event (1) is not open, (3) returns the ball to (5), (4) cuts up to the high post area, (1) becomes the offside low post man, and the continuity goes on. (See Diagram 6-20.)

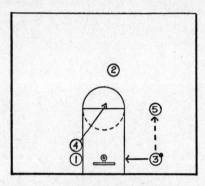

Diagram 6-20

THE WING CLEAR CONTINUITY

Against some defenses, the point man, (1), sometimes dribbles directly at a wing man. In Diagram 6-21, this tells wing man, (2), to clear down and under the post on the offside. The offside wing man, (3), then cuts to the ballside low post area.

The ball is then passed to (4) in the middle. When this happens, (2) cuts out to the offside wing position and (5) slides down to the low post. (4) may shoot, hit (5) or (3) in the layup slots, or reverse the ball to (2) for a jump shot. (See Diagram 6-22.)

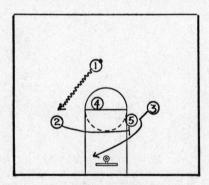

Diagram 6-21

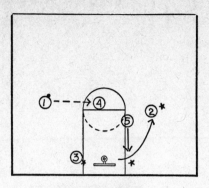

Diagram 6-22

THE OUTSIDE CUT CONTINUITY

When (1) passes to a wing, as he did to (3) in Diagram 6-23, and makes an outside cut, another continuity is set in motion. Again, the offside wing man, (2), comes out front for defensive balance. The two post men, (4) and (5), follow this rule: (a) "If you are the nearest post man to the ball, cut to the ballside corner and create an overload (See (5) in Diagram 6-23.); (b) If you are the offside post man, cut to the ball side. (See (4) in Diagram 6-23.) Cut to a hole in the zone if possible."

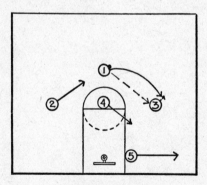

Diagram 6-23

Wing man, (3), now returns the ball to (1) and cuts through the zone. (See Diagram 6-24.) Player (1) may now: (a) pass to (4) cutting to the ballside post; (b) utilize the triangle made possible by

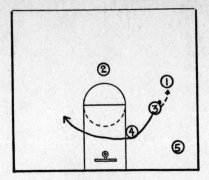

Diagram 6-24

(5)'s cut to the corner; or (c) reverse the ball by way of (2) to (3), who cuts through the zone. In this event, (2) has the option of making an outside cut and again keying the continuity. (See Diagrams 6-25 and 6-26.)

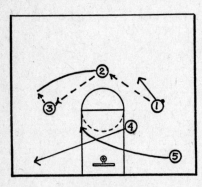

Diagram 6-25

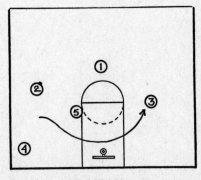

Diagram 6-26

7

THE FULL COURT
PRESSURE GAME OFFENSE

Many games are won or lost because of a team's rotation to defensive pressure. Today's teams are masters at applying defenses that may be zone or man-to-man in nature and may involve full, three-fourths, or half court pressure. Also, many teams apply multiple pressure games that vary the length and type of defense and are keyed by such things as made free throws, made field goals, or even defensive huddles. Because of this upsurge in the number of teams using pressure defenses, a well-prepared team must have offensive plans to counter them. Following are a variety of ideas which will provide methods to attack defensive pressure from many angles.

TWO PHASE PRESS OFFENSE

The first decision you must make when deciding how your team will face pressure defenses is whether they will: (1) attempt to

"Blitz" the pressure team by taking the ball out quickly and forcing it right to the basket; or (2) take their time and pick the defense apart with a deliberate pattern.

Blitzing the press

If they should decide to blitz the defense, the pattern they run should be very similar to their fast break plan. If the defense is a zone press, dribbling should be kept to a minimum. If it is man-to-man, the ball should be given to the best ball handlers, and they should be given room to work. A good example of an adjustable blitz plan to use after the opposition has scored is as follows:

A. VERSUS ZONE PRESSES

As soon as the ball goes through the basket, the center, (5), goes to get it and both forwards, (3) and (4), step out of bounds on their respective sides of the court. The center passes the ball quickly to one of the forwards, (4) in Diagram 7-1, and the guard on that side of the court, (2), wings to the outlet area. The offside guard, (1), cuts to the center of the court, stops, pivots, and faces the ball. The center, (5), drifts to the free throw line. If the pass can be made to the outlet man, (2), the offside forward, (3), cuts down the far sideline. The outlet man, (2), attempts to get the ball to the guard at mid-court, (1), who looks for the offside forward and the outlet man, (2), who released and went downcourt after he got the ball into the middle. (See Diagram 7-2.) The outlet man may also throw a cross court pass to the forward moving down the far sideline. (See Diagram 7-3.) This is possible because the zone will concentrate on covering the ball side of the court.

If the outlet man, (2), is not open, the forward with the ball has two choices—he may pass to the center, who then gets the ball to the offside forward, (3), on the weak side. (See Diagram 7-4.) If (3) senses trouble and can't dribble, he looks for (1) in the middle, who attempts to get the ball to either (2) or (4) on the now weak side. (See Diagram 7-5.) Or, the inbounding forward, (4), may pass the ball to the weakside forward, who also is out of bounds. All this does is reverse the assignments of the players. Guard (1) becomes the outlet man and (2) cuts to the middle and sets up a pivot. (See Diagram 7-6.)

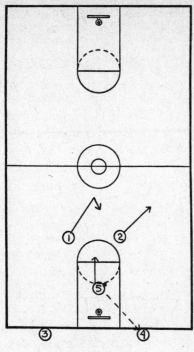

Diagram 7-1

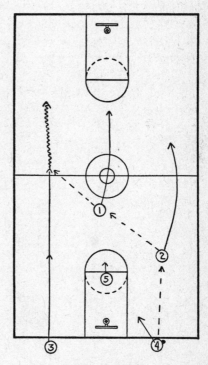

Diagram 7-2

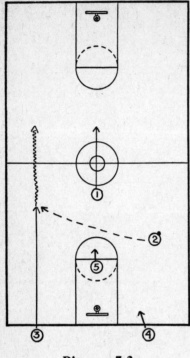

Diagram 7-3

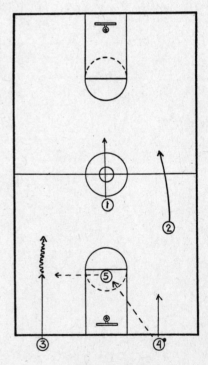

Diagram 7-4

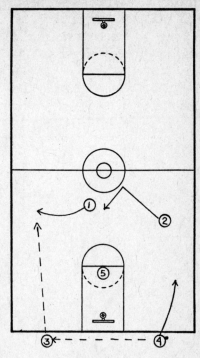

Diagram 7-6

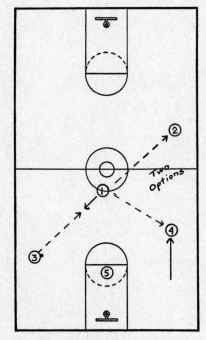

Diagram 7-5

This is a very good move, and it forces the defense to make a very radical adjustment.

(*Note*: The center, (5), is the safety valve man and trails the play downcourt, helping when he must. It is also possible to release the center as soon as he gets the ball to a forward out of bounds. This eliminates one of the options but prevents the defensive safety man from playing too close to mid-court See Diagram 7-7.)

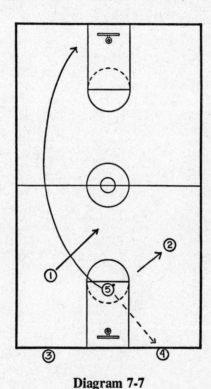

Diagram 7-7

B. BLITZING THE MAN-TO-MAN PRESS

Versus man-to-man pressure, the post man, (5), releases as soon as he makes the pass out of bounds. (See Diagram 7-7.) The inbounding forward looks first for the outlet man, (2), on the sideline. If he cannot get him the ball, the outlet man cuts to the center and the guard in the middle of the court loops to the ball side.

(See Diagram 7-8.) If the inbounds man can get the ball to the guards, he passes to his counterpart on the weak side, who looks for (2) cutting toward him. (See Diagram 7-9.)

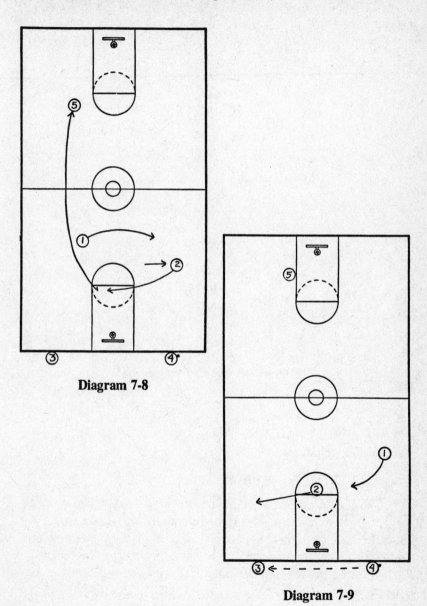

Diagram 7-8

Diagram 7-9

Once the ball has been inbounded, the guards, (1) and (2), bring it upcourt. The offside forward, (4), clears down the sideline, and the inbounding forward, (3), trails the play and acts as the safety valve. (See Diagram 7-10.)

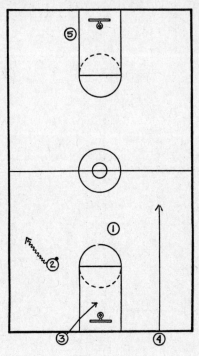

Diagram 7-10

The deliberate pattern

A. VERSUS ZONE PRESSURE

Basically, against a full court zone press, the deliberate offensive team should attempt to spread the defense, get the ball in the middle and then to the unguarded weak side. As they are doing this, they must at all times look downcourt to make sure the defense is not cheating up too high. If they are, the offense must long pass them.

This deliberate pattern starts with both guards, (1) and (2), out of bounds on their respective sides of the court and both forwards, (3) and (4), at mid-court. The center, (5) may be in either of the places. He may release and go all the way downcourt, or set up between the mid-court circle and backcourt free throw circle facing the ball. (See Diagrams 7-11 and 7-12.)

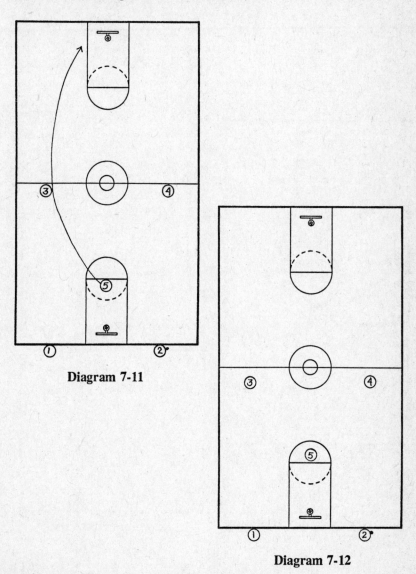

Diagram 7-11

Diagram 7-12

He, (5), must make his move quickly because his position on the court will determine the assignments of the forwards, (3) and (4). If (5) clears downcourt, the forwards have this rule: "When the ball is on your side, cut to the sideline; when it is on the opposite side, cut to the middle." (For an example, see Diagram 7-13.)

If the post man, (5), sets up between the two backcourt circles facing the ball, the forwards have this rule: "When you are on the ball side, come to the ball and at least be in the front court; when the ball is on the opposite side, you should be in the back court and present the threat of a long pass." (See Diagram 7-14 for an example.)

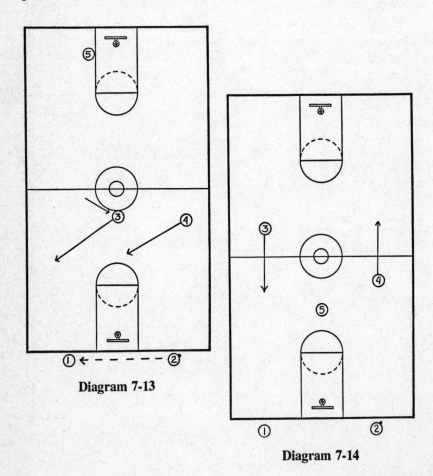

Diagram 7-13

Diagram 7-14

Once the center key has been learned, the same basic pattern may be run from either alignment. The inbounding guard, (2) in Diagram 7-15, attempts to make a penetration pass to either the man on his side or the man in the middle. If he, (2), cannot make the penetration pass, he passes the ball to the other guard, (1), who is also out of bounds. (Note: As soon as this pass is made, the original inbounding guard must step inbounds.) (1) then attempts to make a penetrating pass to his side man or to the man in the middle. If the pass-in is made to the side man, he attempts to get it into the middle. Once a penetrating pass is made, the offside guard will cut down the offside sideline and usually be wide open. When the middle man gets the ball, he must look for the offside guard and also be aware of what is happening downcourt. Diagram 7-15 shows the pattern with the center release and Diagram 7-16 shows the pattern with the center posting.

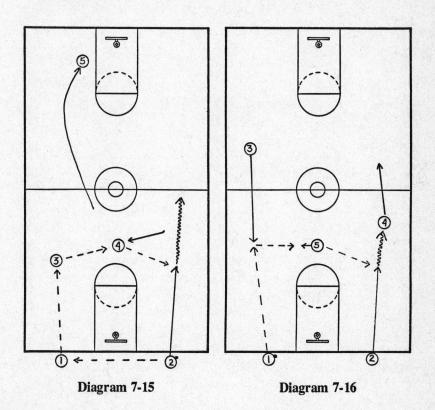

Diagram 7-15   Diagram 7-16

(*Note*: In either of the two phases, the guard who made the penetration pass is the back man.)

B. VERSUS MAN-TO-MAN PRESSURE

When playing against man-to-man pressure, it must be understood that although you have a team plan, there will be times when it becomes a man-on-man situation. A coach must never neglect honing the skills of his guards in regard to one-on-one and two-on-two plays.

It is often a very functional idea to use part of your regular man-to-man offense as a full court, man-to-man pressure offense. For example, three man-to-man offensive plays that work very well against full court pressure are—The Split Play, The Backdoor Play, and The High Post Slash.

(*Note*: Versus man-to-man pressure, the post man stays in the backcourt.)

THE SPLIT PLAY

This play is keyed by a pass from the guard who received the inbounds pass, (2), to the post man, (5), setting up just in the back court. As the pass is made, the onside forward, (4), backdoors his man. (See Diagram 7-17.)

The guards then split the post with the passing guard, (2), going first. The post man, (5), looks first for (4) on the back door, next for (1) coming off (2), and then for (2) going over the top of a definite screen set by forward, (3). (See Diagram 7-18.)

THE BACKDOOR PLAY

This play is keyed when the center, (5), breaks up and to the ball side, and the offside forward, (3), to the center position. (3) then receives a bounce pass from guard, (2), and guard, (1), backdoors his man. (See Diagram 7-19.)

If (1) is not open, he keeps going and clears out. This gives (2) the option of being the second guard through or going over a double screen formed by (5) and (4). (See Diagram 7-20.)

If (3) can't hit (1) or (2) on their cuts, they hook back and (3) passes to one of them in the front court.

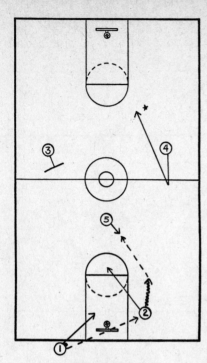

Diagram 7-17

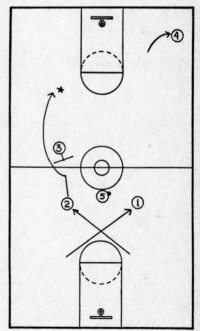

Diagram 7-18

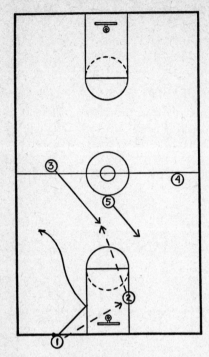

Diagram 7-19

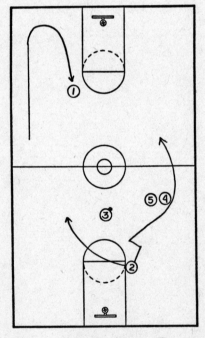

Diagram 7-20

THE HIGH POST SLASH

This play starts with a pass from (2) to the onside forward, (4). (2) then slashes off the high post man, (5). (See Diagram 7-21.)

If (1) is not open, he goes to the offside corner. (5) screens opposite for the offside forward who cuts to the hoop, and then to the offside. (See Diagram 7-22.) If neither (2) nor (3) is open, (4) dribbles to the middle and hands off to (1), who changes direction cuts, takes the ball, and penetrates as for as possible. (See Diagram 7-23.)

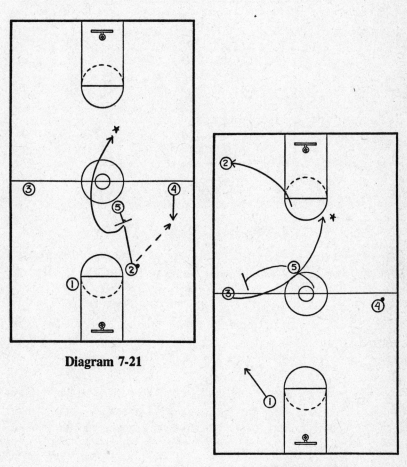

Diagram 7-21

Diagram 7-22

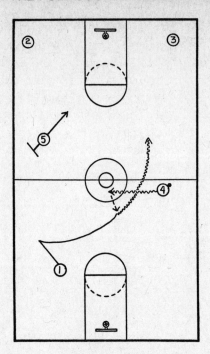

Diagram 7-23

AN ALL PURPOSE PRESSURE OFFENSE

If you are fortunate and have a very agile big man, this pressure offense may be run against either zone or man-to-man, full court pressure defenses. The agile big player, always takes the ball out of bounds after the opposition scores. The two guards, (1) and (2), attempt to get open on their respective sides of the court, and the other two men, (3) and (4), sprint to mid-court and set up wide apart, facing the ball on opposite sides of the court. (See Diagram 7-24.)

As soon as the ball is inbounded to guard, (1), the offside guard, (2), comes to screen (5)'s man as (5) cuts away from the ball. The offside mid-court man, (3), cuts to the center and the ballside mid-court man, (4), goes downcourt to unclutter the back court. (See Diagram 7-25.)

The agile big man, (5), utilizes (2)'s screen and cuts opposite

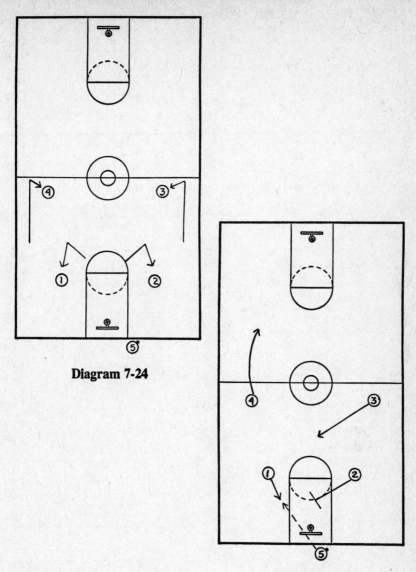

Diagram 7-24

Diagram 7-25

the ball. (1) man now make a cross court pass to (5). (See Diagram 7-26.) Or, (1) may pass to (3) in the middle, who looks for (5) going down the weak side. (See Diagram 7-27.)

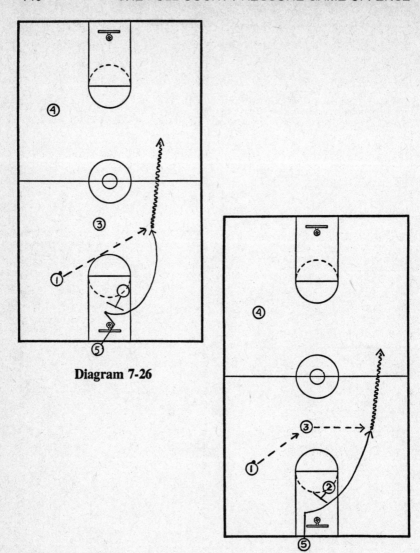

Diagram 7-26

Diagram 7-27

(*Note*: In either situation, the agile big man, (5), would then bring the ball into front court.

After passing to (3), (1) splits the post with (2). (See Diagram 7-28.)

If the defense is switching or playing zone, (1) and (2) fake the split. (2) then cuts down his sideline, and the passer, (1), changes direction and comes back to the ball for a safety valve pass from (3). (See Diagram 7-29.)

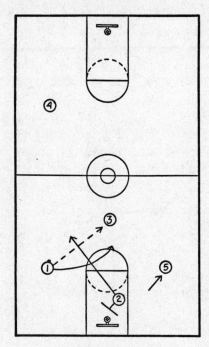

Diagram 7-28

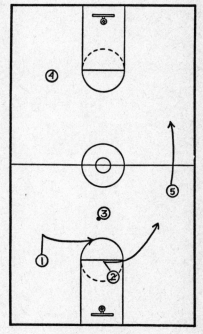

Diagram 7-29

Inbounding procedures

If you are having difficulty getting the ball inbounds, the following techniques may be used.

Free throw line stack

As the agile big man, (5), retrieves the ball from the basket, steps out of bounds and looks for an open teammate, the two guards, (1) and (2), and one of the forwards, (3), form a stack along, and parallel to, the free throw line. The other forward, (4), goes to the mid-court area. (See Diagram 7-30.)

The guards use their own initiative by either crossing or faking the cross and coming to their respective sides of the court. At the same time, (3) goes to screen for the mid-court man, (4). (4) cuts to the head of the key and (3) rolls downcourt to either side. (See

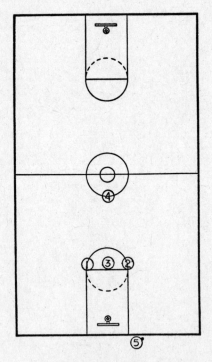

Diagram 7-30

Diagram 7-31.) From here, (5) simply inbounds the ball to the open man, and goes opposite to start the pattern. (See Diagram 7-32.)

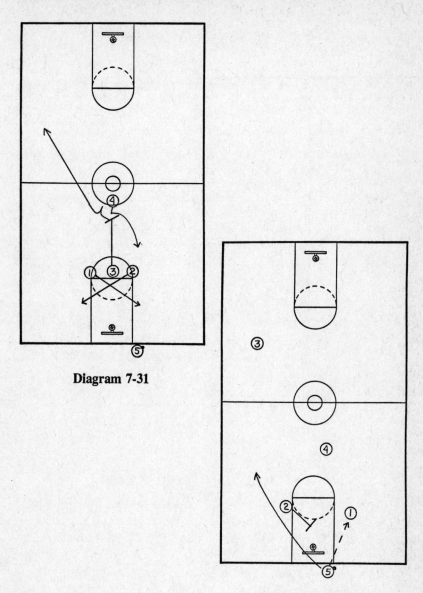

Diagram 7-31

Diagram 7-32

Forward screen

Another method of freeing an inbounds receiver is to have the forwards screen for the guard on their side and roll to the mid-court area. (See Diagram 7-33.)

Again, from here, (5) passes the ball in and goes opposite to start the pattern.

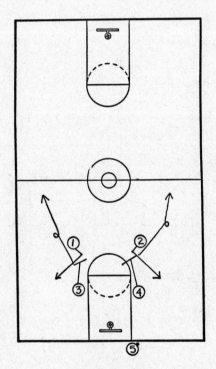

Diagram 7-33

A HALF COURT ZONE PRESS PATTERN

This pattern begins as the ball is passed to one of the forwards by the guard on his side. In Diagram 7-34, guard, (1), passes to forward, (3). This tells the offside guard, (2), to cut through to the offside low post area.

The cut by (2) also keys the offside forward, (4), to cut to the high post area.

After making the penetration pass, (1) must change direction and move to the middle of the court. It also helps if the low post man, (5), moves out a couple of steps toward the corner. (See Diagram 7-35.)

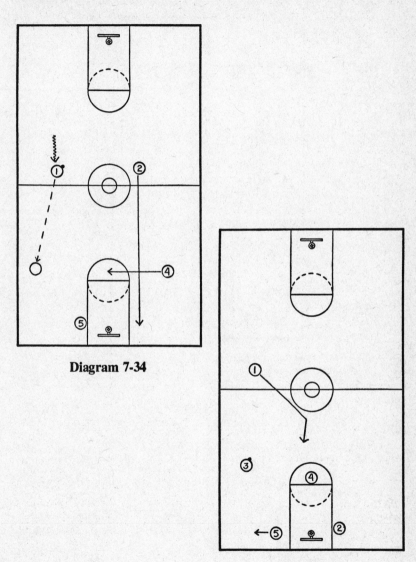

Diagram 7-34

Diagram 7-35

The first option is to get the ball to (4) in the middle. If this can be done, either (5) or (2) will usually be open in their respective lay-up slots. (See Diagram 7-36.)

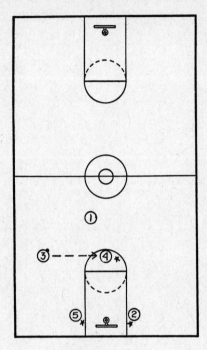

Diagram 7-36

If (4) is not open, (3) may look for (5) in the low post area or reverse the ball by way of (1). When this happens, (2) moves up to the wing position and receives the ball from (1). From here, the man in the high post area, (4), slides down to the ballside low post area. The now offside wing man, (3), then cuts to the high post area. (See Diagram 7-37.)

From here, the same options prevail. (2) may pass the ball into the middle, pass the ball into the new low post man, (4), or reverse it to (5) by way of (1). When it is reversed, (3) slides from high to low and the offside wing man, (2), cuts to the high post. (See Diagram 7-38.) (*Note*: At all times, the number one objective is to

get the ball into the high post area, where the receiver may shoot or
pass to the people in the lay-up slots.)

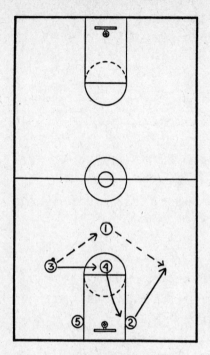

Diagram 7-37

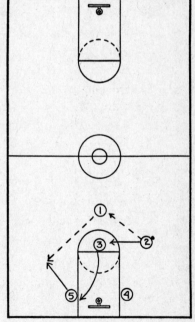

Diagram 7-38

COACHING POINTS

Whatever style or pattern you decide on, you must condition your players to the fact that, at best, the pressure defense is a gamble. Much practice time should be devoted to the pressure game until your players understand it and feel confident against it. Some of the individual fundamentals to be stressed are:

1. Don't waste your dribble.
2. Don't get out of control when dribbling.
3. Try to throw passes that penetrate diagonally.
4. Follow your pressure game plan.
5. Know where the traps are.
6. Hit the first open man.
7. Remember, the ball must touch a player on the court five seconds after it is given to the inbounder.
8. Look downcourt.
9. Split the double-team.
10. Use the two hand overhead pass when under pressure.
11. You have ten seconds in the back court, and it is a long time.
12. Jump balls are better than lost balls.
13. Do not dribble into the front court and stop near the mid-court area.
14. Get the ball in the middle.
15. Don't throw a cross the lane pass at your defensive basket.
16. Keep your eye on the ball at all times.
17. When you are double-teamed, someone must be open.
18. Move the ball forward whenever possible.
19. Be moving toward the passer when you receive the ball.
20. Make a lot of ball fakes.

8

UTILIZING THE FAST BREAK

The secret to the fast break game is to have simple, flexible options that allow you to get the ball downcourt by the fastest, safest method, and enable you to outnumber the opposition in the scoring area. The following fast break pattern has those attributes.

THE OUTLET PASS

The man who secures the rebound must be taught to turn to the outside and quickly release the ball. This pattern gives the rebounder three release options as shown in Diagram 8-1. The onside guard, (2), cuts to the rebound side and assumes a position that allows him to see most of the entire court. The offside guard, (1), is called the flyer. He releases and sprints downcourt, looking for a possible long pass from (5) for a lay-up.

If the sideline outlet guard, (2), does not receive the ball, he executes a comeback pattern and moves to the center of the court. If none of these outlet options is open, the rebounder, (5), dribbles to the outside and downcourt, and looks for (2) in the middle. (2) must be taught to wait for the ball. (See Diagram 8-2.)

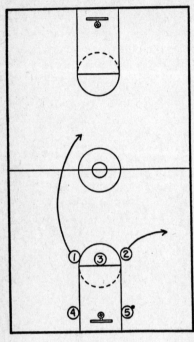

Diagram 8-1

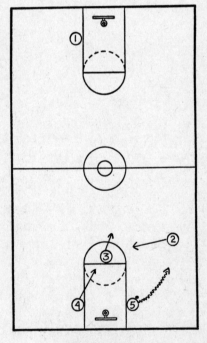

Diagram 8-2

LANE ORGANIZATION

The "bouncing" guard

To use this method, the guard, (1), who "flew" as his team secured the rebound, goes all the way to the baseline and then bounces on the same side free throw line high. (*Note:* If the rebound would have come to the other side of the court, the guards would change assignments.) The guard who took the outlet pass on the sideline, (2), then dribbles to the middle and downcourt. This leaves only one lane open. The three inside men are instructed to run for the lane in which the outlet pass was received. The first of the three to get there fills the lane, the second is the trailer, and the third is the safety man. (See Diagram 8-3.)

The secret to this phase of the break is to have guards who are deadly jump shooters from 12 to 15 feet out. Outlet guard, (2), is told to look for the flying guard (who has "bounced" out) as he

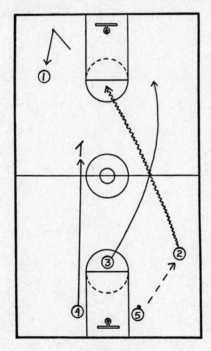

Diagram 8-3

dribbles downcourt. (See Diagram 8-4.) Usually, the flying guard, (1), is open for a jump shot because people defending against the fast break are told to retreat to the basket. If (1) is not open, (2) dribbles to the free throw line and looks for the runner in the other lane, or for a jump shot. (See Diagram 8-5.) If neither is open, he passes to the flyer, (1), and clears the lane for the trailer, (4). (See Diagram 8-6.)

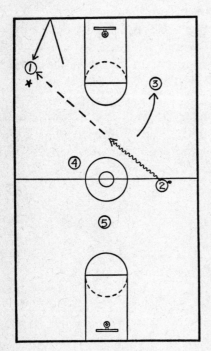

Diagram 8-4

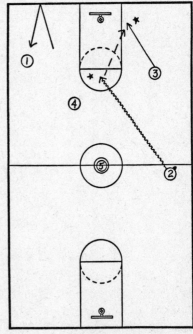

Diagram 8-5

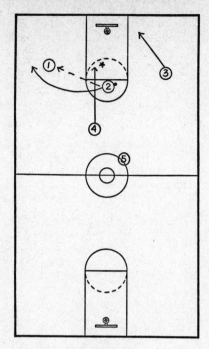

Diagram 8-6

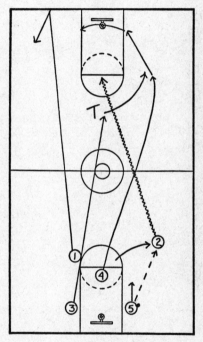

Diagram 8-7

THE RUNNER'S LANE TRAILER

Another method of utilizing a trailer is to have the first man in the runner's lane make his cut and then clear. As shown in Diagram 8-7, (4) was the first man in the runner's lane. After his cut to the basket, he cleared to the opposite side of the lane and made room for trailer, (3), to fill the runner's lane as shown in Diagram 8-8.

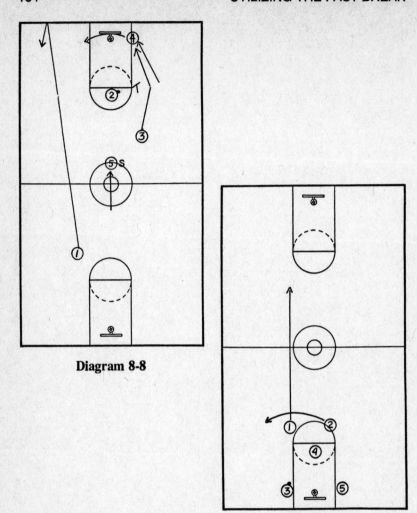

Diagram 8-8

Diagram 8-9

A PERSONNEL ADJUSTMENT

If a team is blessed with a "pure" shooter ((1) in Diagram 8-9), it may be to their advantage to have him "fly" on every play. This requires the other guard, (2), to wait for the outlet pass on every play. If he, (2), also happens to be an outstanding dribbler, this is the type of personnel for the adjustment.

As shown in Diagram 8-9, the pure shooter, (1), flies in spite of the fact that the outlet pass will come out on his side and (2), the ball handler, crosses over to take the outlet pass.

(*Note:* An additional advantage of having a flyer arises when the opposition is working for the last-second shot. If one of your players secures the rebound, he knows the flyer is downcourt, and you might get the last show to win a close game.)

ALTERNATE PATTERN

This fast break method is similar, but the flying guard does not always bounce. He may cross over to the outlet side corner. Also, the forwards stay in the lane on their side of the court, and the center is always the safety man. The scoring options are very much the same.

In Diagram 8-10, Center, (5), secures the rebound and looks for the outlet man, (2), and the flyer, (1). After the outlet is made to

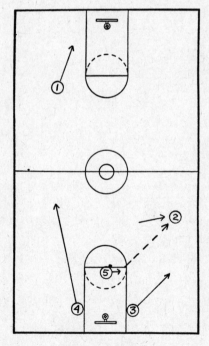

Diagram 8-10

guard, (2), he again dribbles to the middle, looking for the now crossing guard. (See Diagram 8-11.)

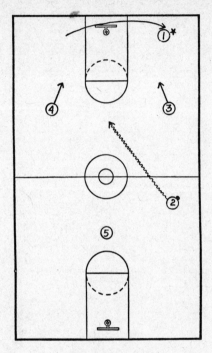

Diagram 8-11

If (1) is not open coming across, (2) continues to the free throw line and may jump shoot, pass to (4) or (3) in the outside lanes, or to the flyer coming out free throw line high. (See Diagram 8-12.)

The trailer phase comes when the guard-to-guard pass is made. Dribbling guard, (2), clears the lane and, if the defense goes out to cover (1), the player in the ballside lane, (3), is often open for a trailer lay-up. (See Diagram 8-13.)

When using this method, the center, (5), is the back man (safety).

After the opposition scores

When the opposition scores, the same pattern is run, but with these alterations: The post man, (5), always takes the ball out of

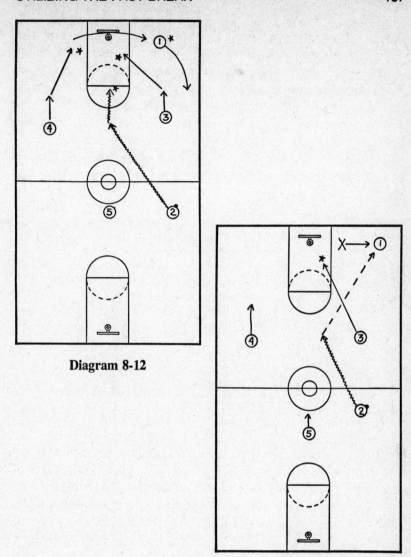

Diagram 8-12

Diagram 8-13

bounds on the right-hand side, facing up-court. The ballside guard, (1), waits for the outlet pass on that side, and the offside guard, (2), flies. It is very important to remember to have the better ball handling guard on the outlet side and the shooter, flying. It is very seldom that the flying guard, (2), is open for a long pass from (5), but he is open quite often for a jump shot after he has "bounced." After a score, players going back on defense usually run back to the lane area before coming out to pick up their men. Since the forwards involved in this fast break pattern, (3) and (4), are instructed to run all the way to the basket in their lane, they tend to freeze the defenders in the lane and give (2) a chance to bounce out for an unmolested jump shot. Player (5), after taking the ball out of bounds, trails the play upcourt in the event that (1) must pick up his dribble. (See Diagram 8-14.)

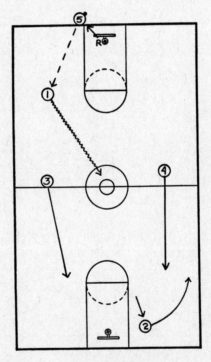

Diagram 8-14

It is also a very effective idea to have the flying guard, (2), cross over to the outlet side corner. The guard receiving the outlet pass, (1), is then instructed to get the ball to the flyer as soon as he can. The defenders downcourt are faced with the dilemma of whether to go out after the shooter in the corner, or stay in and cover the high percentage scoring area. (See Diagram 8-15.)

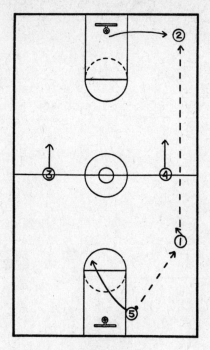

Diagram 8-15

EARLY OFFENSE

Early offense is a method of running a simple, basic play after the break has ended but before the defense is organized. Using the bouncing guard method of lane organization, the following is an example of early offense: When (2) diagnoses that none of the primary fast break options are open, he passes to the bouncing guard and clears the lane for the trailer play. His method of clearing the lane will be one of the three early offensive plays. Player (2) may pass to (1) and come and screen for him. (See Diagram 8-16.)

Then they work a simple screen and roll play. Player (2) may pass to (1) and cut outside him. (1) will hand off and roll to the basket. (2) may shoot or look for (1) rolling. (See Diagram 8-17.)

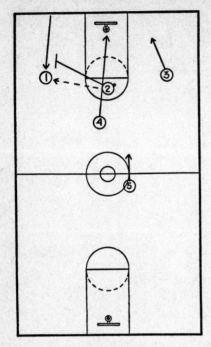

Diagram 8-16

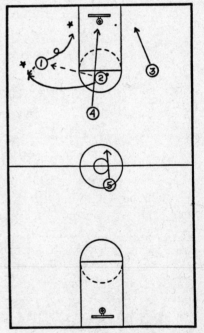

Diagram 8-17

Player (2) also may pass to (1) and screen opposite for the man who came down in that lane. (See Diagram 8-18.)

This option works particularly well, because, when the trailer (4) goes through, it flattens out the defense and leaves the head of the key area open.

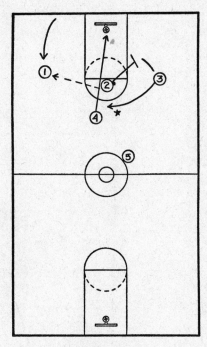

Diagram 8-18

FAST BREAK DRILLS

Outlet drill

This drill is designed to teach the outlet and lane organization phases of the fast break. It uses four offensive men and one defender. There are two rebounders, one on each side of the backboard, and two outlet men. The outlet men are a step higher than the head of the key and as wide apart as the free throw lane. The one defender, X^1, is between the guards and the midcourt line.

The coach starts the drill by throwing the ball off the backboard to one of the rebounders. The offside guard flies and the onside guard goes to the outlet area. From here, the rebounder's pass will be determined by what the defender does. If the defender retreats, the rebounder hits the outlet man, and a three-on-one fast break is run. (See Diagram 8-19.) If the defender attempts to steal the outlet pass, the rebounder must read this and pass long to the flyer. (See Diagram 8-20.)

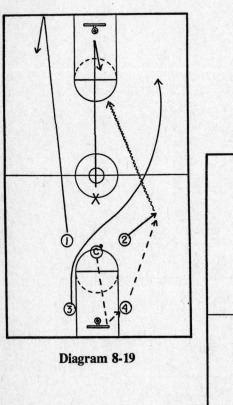

Diagram 8-19

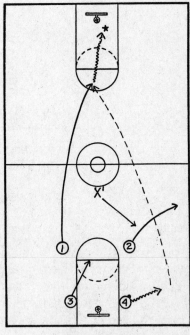

Diagram 8-20

Touchdown pass drill

Many games are determined by the success or failure of a long pass thrown late in the game. This drill provides practice in throwing and catching that pass, and also teaches the flyer to bounce and make the 12 to 15 foot jump shot. There is a line of players under the basket at each end of the court. The ball is given to the second man in one of the lines. The first man in line sprints downcourt and receives a baseball pass. The second man in the other line takes the ball as it comes through the basket and passes to the first man in his line, who has sprinted downcourt. From here, the passer becomes the next runner. (See Diagram 8-21.) This part of the drill continues until the team has made 25 consecutive lay-ups. After that, the flyer goes downcourt to the baseline, then comes back to receive the pass for a 12 to 15 foot jump shot. (See Diagram 8-22.)

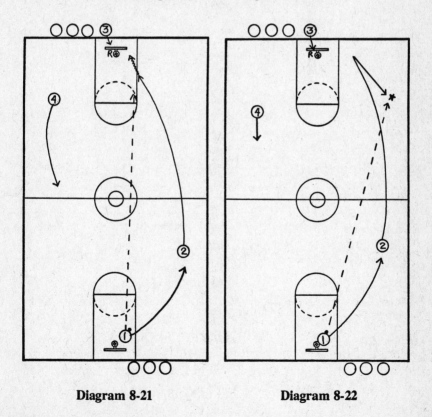

Diagram 8-21   **Diagram 8-22**

(*Note*: After (2) shoots, (3) retrieves the rebound and looks for the new flyer, (4), after he has bounced.)

Middle man out

The majority of the team is in three lines facing downcourt at one end of the gym. The middle man of the first three in line has the ball. Two defenders are in a tandem fast break defensive alignment at the far end of the court as in Diagram 8-23. The ball is given to a

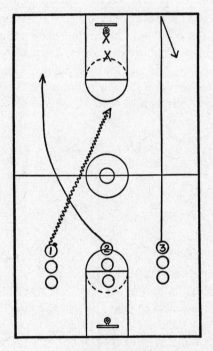

Diagram 8-23

man in an outside lane who dribbles to the middle. The man in the far outside lane, (3), "flies" and bounces, and the middle lane man, (2), sprints and fills the ballside lane as per the 3-on-2 fast break pattern. As soon as the fast break is over, either by the offense's scoring or the defense's securing the ball via a steal or rebound, the middle man of the fast break, (1), drops out and returns to the end of the lines at the opposite end of the court. (See Diagram 8-24.)

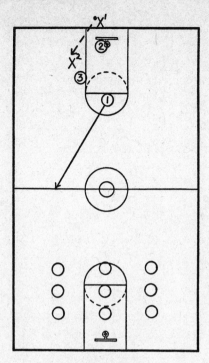

Diagram 8-24

The two outside lane fast break men, (2) and (3), now become defensive men and the former defensive tandem, X^1 and X^2, move to the offense. If the fast break trio scored, the ball must be taken out of bounds. If not, the defense runs a fast break. The new offensive men must now get the ball to mid-court against the two defenders. If they don't make it, they stay on defense. If they do make it, the two defensive men who were the outside lane fast breakers retreat to the fast break defensive tandem.

Versus defensive pressure (two versus three)

During the practice week that precedes a game with a team that plays very strong pressure defense, it might be wise to make the following adjustment in this drill: once defenders, X^1 and X^2 have obtained the ball, instead of having the middle man, (1), drop out, have him retreat to the head of the key with instructions to disallow any long passes and to stop dribblers that have broken loose. For example, in Diagram 8-25, the former middle man, (1), waits while defenders, (3) and (2), pressure X^1 and X^2. In this case, X^1 beat (3) and would have been open for a pass downcourt, but he was picked up by (1). This forces X^1 to come back to the ball, which is a very important move to make against a pressure defense. (See Diagram 8-26.) During the interim, X^2 must protect the ball and look for X^1 to come back. If X^2 dribbles and gets free, (1) must stop him. (See Diagram 8-27.)

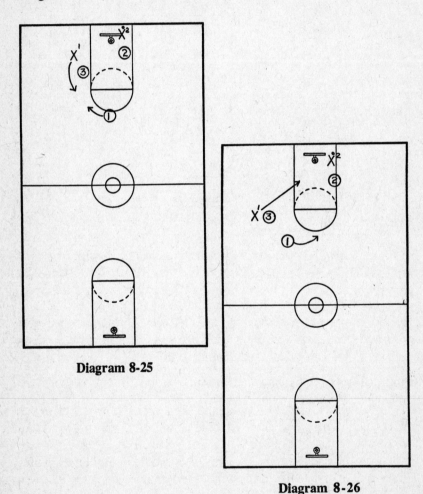

Diagram 8-25

Diagram 8-26

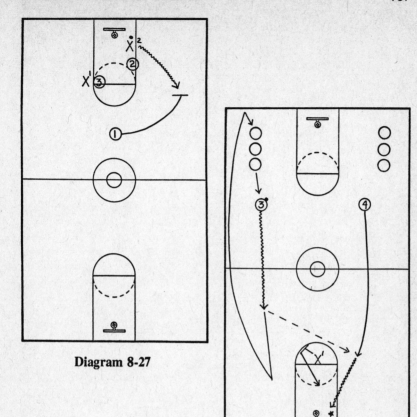

Diagram 8-27

Diagram 8-28

Two-on-one fast break

The same drill may be run from a two-on-one situation. The coach simply designates that the player in one of the fast break lines will drop out and the other line will always play defense. After the fast break defender has acquired the ball, it now is a one-on-one situation, and is very good practice at dribbling the ball upcourt versus pressure.

In Diagram 8-28, the man in the right lane, (3), drops out, and the man in the left lane, (4), plays the defense. (See Diagrams 8-28 and 8-29.)

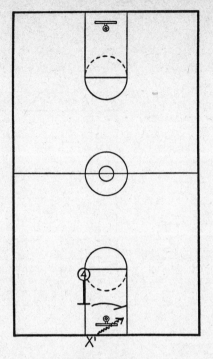

Diagram 8-29

"Call your name" drill

This drill starts with the majority of the team in three lines facing downcourt. The other three players are facing the men in the three lines and are on defense, with one in the middle of the court and one in each of the two outside lanes. The coach is on the end line with the ball. He may throw the ball to either of the outside lanes. When he does this, he calls the name of one of the three defenders, who must come to the end line before going back to defend against the coming fast break. (See X^3 in Diagram 8-30.) The other two defensive men, X^1 and X^2, retreat to the far foul lane. From here, the fast break pattern is run. The man with the ball, (1), dribbles to the middle. The man in the middle lane, (2), goes to the dribbler's side and fills that outside lane. The man in the far outside lane, (3), is the flyer who goes to the far baseline in his lane and bounces.

The dribbler, X^1, may pass to the "bouncer" for a jump shot, jump shoot, or pass to player (2), who sprints to fill the runner's lane. If the break does not develop before X^3 arrives, the defensive men each take a man, and a three-on-three situation results. (See Diagram 8-31.)

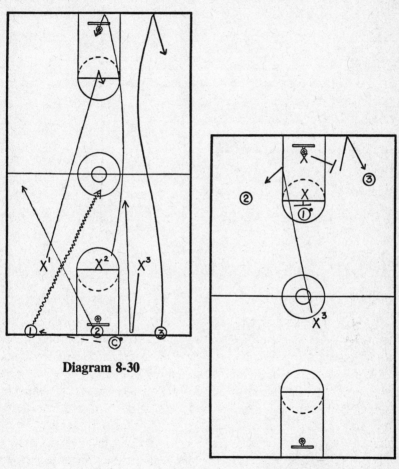

Diagram 8-30

Diagram 8-31

If the offensive team scores, the same three men stay on defense. If the offense does not score, they become the defenders, and the three former defenders go to the end of the offensive lines.

Three man skeleton drill

This drill allows repeated practice of many of the components of the previously presented fast break pattern. It begins with a player, (1), taking a jump shot from the side, a rebounder, (2), waiting to retrieve the shot, and a player, (3), in the same floor position as (1), but on the opposite side of the court. (See Diagram 8-32.)

As soon as (2) retrieves the shot, he turns to the outside. In Diagram 8-33, he turns toward (3)'s side. This makes (3) the outlet man and (1), the flyer. (3) takes the outlet pass and dribbles to the middle and downcourt to the free throw line. The rebounder, (2), runs hard and fills the outlet pass side lane.

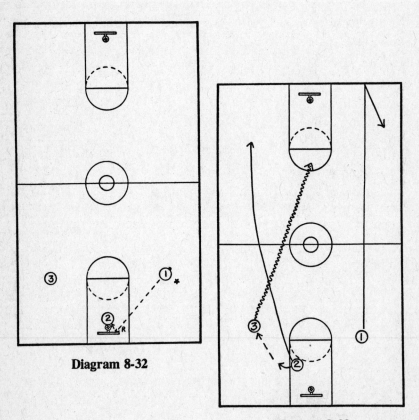

Diagram 8-32

Diagram 8-33

If (2) would have turned to (1)'s side, (1) and (3) would have changed assignments.

From here, one of two things can happen: Middle man, (3), may pass to (1), who has bounced and will take a jump shot. (See Diagram 8-34.)

Or, the middle man, (3), will stop and hit player (2) in the runner's lane for a lay-up shot. (See Diagram 8-35.)

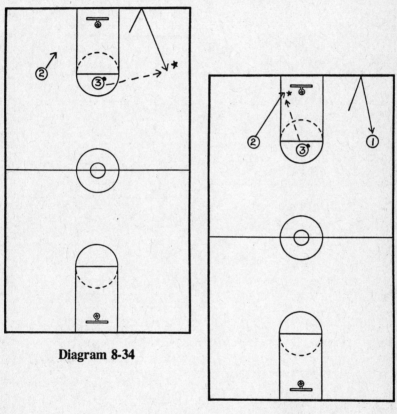

Diagram 8-34

Diagram 8-35

In either case, the middle man will always rebound the shot and start the break in the opposite direction, and the outside lane fillers, (1) and (2), will become potential outlet pass receivers. (See Diagram 8-36.)

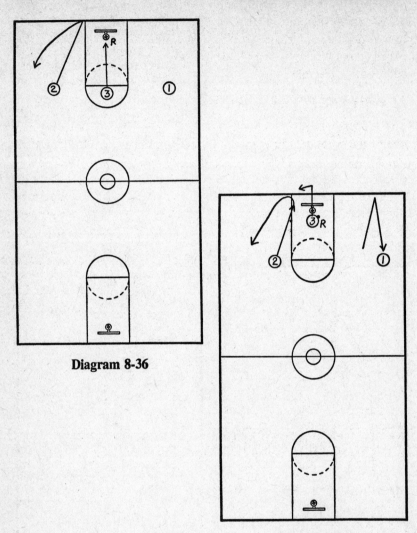

Diagram 8-36

Diagram 8-37

It may appear that the man in the runner's lane ((2) in Diagram 8-37) can't get back in time after he has shot a lay-up on that particular option. To compensate for this, he is taught to make the lay-up and wing back quickly to his outlet area. To make up for this time lapse, the rebounder, (3), must step out of bounds with the ball when a basket is made

(3) may then throw the outlet pass to either side, and one of the two options is run at the opposite end of the court. The same three players run these options up and down the court until they make five consecutive baskets.

HIT THE FLYER (A SPECIAL OPTION)

To practice the flyer option, the rebounder, (3), turns toward one of the potential outlet men ((1), in Diagram 8-38.) This releases the offside man, (2), to fly. When the long pass is thrown, the flyer, (2), makes the lay-up, takes the ball out of bounds, and passes to either of the potential outlet men, (1) and (3), who have trailed him downcourt on their respective sides of the court. (See Diagram 8-39.) The drill then continues.

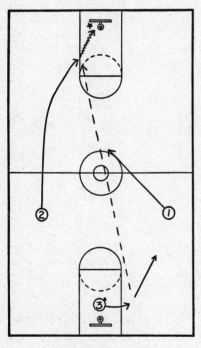

Diagram 8-38

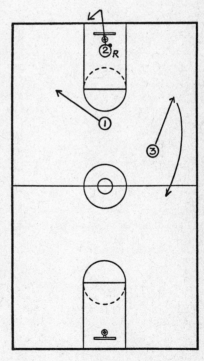

Diagram 8-39

4-on-2 drill

   This drill begins with the players in the positions shown in Diagram 8-40. In Diagram 8-41 the ball is given to (1), who throws a pass to the outlet man on his side, (3). (3) then dribbles to the middle and (2) fills the runner's lane. The offside outlet man, (4), flies and bounces. (1) is the trailer. These four men attempt to score against the defenders, (5) and (6), using the options of the fast break pattern.

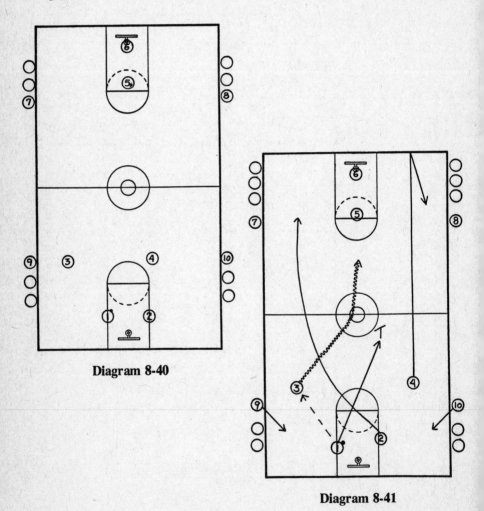

Diagram 8-40

Diagram 8-41

When the defense acquires the ball, either by a steal, rebound, or after a score, an outlet pass is thrown. At this time, the former offensive players, (1), (2), (3), and (4), go to the end of the lines at that end of the court. In Diagram 8-42, defender (6) throws the outlet pass to the man on his side of the court, (8). (8) then dribbles to the middle, (5) fills the runner's lane, and the offside outlet man, (7), is the flyer. This makes player (6) the trailer. These four then make a four-on-two fast break play against the next two defenders, (9) and (10). (See Diagram 8-42.) The two fast break defenders always come from the lines at that respective end of the court.

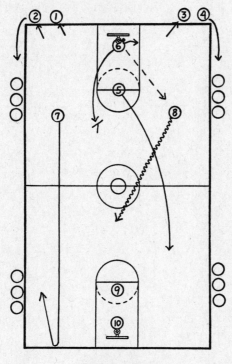

Diagram 8-42

9

CREATING SPECIAL
SITUATION PRESSURE

Special situations may include out of bounds plays, jump ball plays, tip-off plays, last-second shot plays, and the free throw play. When a special situation arises and a team needs a basket or at least ball possession to stay in the game, the coach must decide between execution and surprise. He may decide to run a part of his offense and implore his players to execute to perfection, or, he may turn to a plan that is tailor-made for this particular opponent and surprise them by exploiting an obvious weakness they have shown. I feel that a game situation presents too many distractions and too much pressure to do any on the spot introductions of new ideas. So, from my point of view, I would stress that the special situation plan must, if it is new, come from the scouting report and be covered during the previous week's practice sessions. Following are several special situation plans that have been used successfully.

OUT OF BOUNDS UNDER THE BASKET
(VS. MAN-TO-MAN OR ZONE DEFENSES)

Triangle formation

SCREEN FOR THE SCREENER

Three players, (3), (4), and (5), line up in a triangle, the apex of which is at the free throw line. The fourth man, (2), is two steps from the top of the key. The fifth man, (1), is taking the ball out of bounds. The base player on the ball-side, (5), starts the play by screening for the man on the free throw line, (3), who changes direction and uses the screen. (See Diagram 9-1.) The offside base player, (4), watches (5) set his screen and then screens (5)'s man, who is probably loosening up to help X^3 get over. (4) then rolls down the middle. This is, in effect, screening for the screener, and works very well if timed correctly. (2), at the head of the key, is the safety valve man who is back on defense if the ball is lost, and cuts to the ball after the play has not worked. (See Diagram 9-2.)

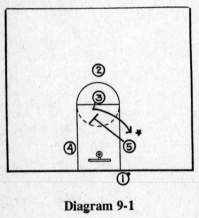

Diagram 9-1

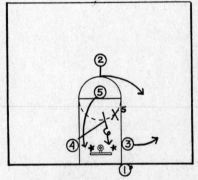

Diagram 9-2

BASELINE CLEAR

In this option, the onside base man, (5), again calls the play. This time he backs out and clears the lay-up slot on that side. This tells (2) to change direction and cut off the apex man, (3), into the open area. (See Diagram 9-3.) If (2) is not open, (4) again screens for the screener, (3), and rolls down the middle. (See Diagram 9-4.) Again, the thing that happens quite often is that (3)'s defender, X^3, will loosen up to help on (2)'s cut. If (4) really headhunts him, (3) will be open for a lay-up in the offside lay-up slot.

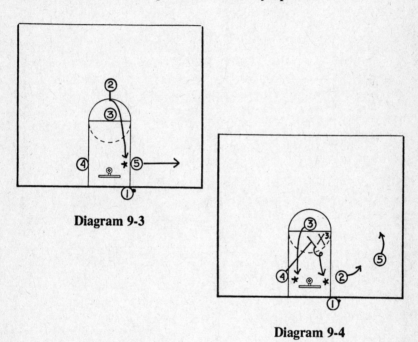

Diagram 9-3

Diagram 9-4

OFFSIDE WALL

The third option is also very effective against both man-to-man and zone defenses. It, too, is keyed by the player in the onside base position, (5). (5) starts the play by coming across the lane to screen for offside base man, (4). (1) looks first for (4) coming across, and second for (5) rolling back. (See Diagram 9-5.) If neither is open, (1) passes to (2), who has cut toward the ball. (2) looks first for a jump shot and then reverses the ball to (3), who steps back, takes the pass, and looks for inbounder, (1), who comes around a definite screen set by (5). (See Diagram 9-6.) At the same time, (2) pinches in for (4), who comes out for a possible jump shot. (See Diagram 9-7.)

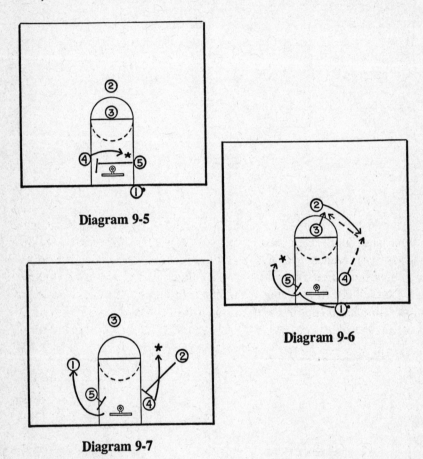

Diagram 9-5

Diagram 9-6

Diagram 9-7

Horizontal line-up

In this formation, (1) takes the ball out; there is one lone man, (5), in the ballside lay-up slot; and three players, (2), (3), and (4), in a line parallel to, and a step above, the free throw line. (See Diagram 9-8.) The lone man, (5), keys the play by his movements. He may spin off, back out, or come up and screen. The other players must read his cut.

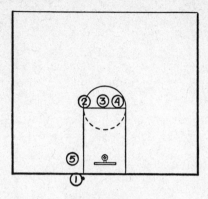

Diagram 9-8

SPIN OFF

In this option, (5) backs into his defender and then spins into the lane, looking for a bounce pass from (1). The offside line-up man, (4), comes over the top to the ballside corner for a possible jump shot. (See Diagram 9-9.) (2) slides into the hole created by (5)'s leaving (this works well versus zone) and (3) backs up for a possible jump shot in the event his man has backed off. If no one is open, the ball is passed to (4) in the corner, out to (3), and then to

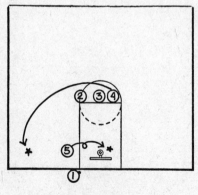

Diagram 9-9

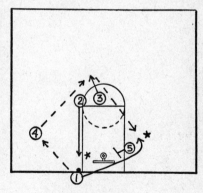

Diagram 9-10

(1), who has gone opposite his pass and utilized a screen set by (5). (See Diagram 9-10.) This last option is called around the horn, and works well versus zones.

BACK OUT

This time, (5) backs out to the ballside corner. (2) crosses in front of (3), creating a natural screen for him as he cuts to the ballside lay-up slot. (See Diagram 9-11.) This is also a good zone option. (4) backs up for a possible jump shot and, if no one is open, the around the horn option is worked for (1). (See Diagram 9-12.)

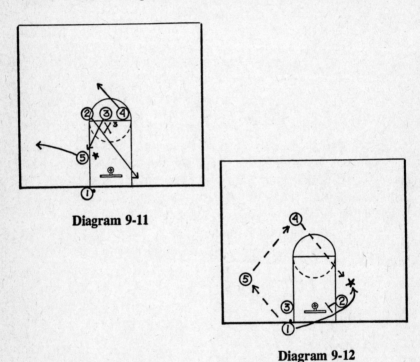

Diagram 9-11

Diagram 9-12

COME UP AND SCREEN

In this option, (5) comes up and blind screens (2)'s defender. (2) cuts for the basket and (5) rolls. (See Diagram 9-13.) (4) cuts to the ballside corner and (3) backs out. If no one is open, the around the horn option is run for (1). (See Diagram 9-14.)

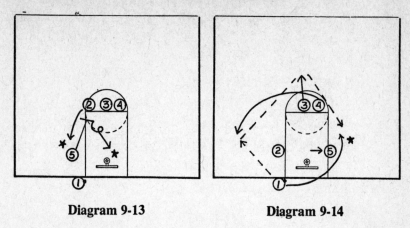

Diagram 9-13   Diagram 9-14

OUT OF BOUNDS ON SIDE (VS MAN-TO-MAN DEFENSES)

Weave play

THE WEAVE OPTION

This three-option play starts with three men out front, including the inbounds passer, and a high double post. When the inbounder, (1), bounces the ball, it tells (2) to screen opposite for (3). (3) then moves toward the ball and (2) stays back for defensive balance. (See Diagram 9-15.) (1) passes to (3) and then moves toward him and receives a return pass. The nearside post man, (5), steps up and screens (3)'s man, and (3) goes over the screen and toward the

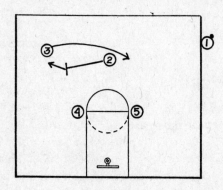

Diagram 9-15

basket. (1) takes a dribble and quickly gets the ball to the offside post man, (4) who immediately shovel passes the ball to (3), who may be open for a lay-up shot. (See Diagram 9-16.)

THE DRIBBLE OPTION

As a change of pace, (1) may, after receiving the ball back from (3), simply work a screen and roll with the offside post man, (4), by dribbling off him, instead of passing to him. (See Diagram 9-17.)

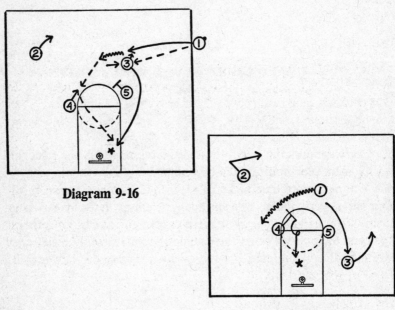

Diagram 9-16

Diagram 9-17

THE LOB OPTION

As the play begins, (2), who starts the play in all situations by going opposite of the inbounder, (1), receives a high screen from the offside post man, (4). (1) then throws a cross court lob to (2) for a possible lay-up shot. If the play has been called ahead of time, (5) can facilitate the play by moving toward the ball and clearing the foul lane area. (See Diagram 9-18.)

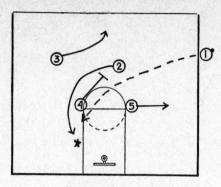

Diagram 9-18

Jump ball play

In his great book, *Power Basketball*, Ed Jucker mentions that there are at least 92 possible jump ball situations. This takes into consideration such factors as the area of floor at which the jump ball is being executed, and the strengths and weaknesses of the jumpers. He also mentions the advantage of creating an open spot on jump balls by attempting to have two consecutive men on the circle and having them block out just like on rebounds.

We have used the open spot method at Eastern Montana College for several years, and do so by putting the burden on our guards. We designate one guard to always attempt to create the open spot, and the other to be responsible for defensive balance. If either of the guards is jumping, he designates a forward to do his job. Usually, it is the small forward.

Tip-off plays

Many coaches have given up on tip-off plays and feel it is more realistic to simply concentrate on obtaining the ball, and then on running your offense. I have not, as yet, come to this position, and my teams have gotten some easy baskets with the following plan.

Again, the guards are the key men. The safety guard, (1), is again responsible for defensive balance. He always lines up behind our center.

The remainder of the players are in a diamond formation. The big forward, (4), is straight ahead of the jumper; the small forward,

(3), to the center's, (5)'s left; and the other guard, (2), usually the quicker one, to the jumper's right. From here, a determination of our chances to gain the tip-off is made and one of the following calls is in order.

"SURE"

This, of course, is when we feel we will get the tip. The ball is tipped straight ahead to the big forward, (4), and both side men, (2) and (3), go to our basket as soon as he, (4), obtains it. (See Diagram 9-19.)

"SAFE"

The odds are definitely against our obtaining the tip. Our center attempts to tip it straight ahead to (4). Both side men, (2) and (3), attempt to outguess the opposition and steal their tip. The safe guard drops back before the ball is thrown. (See Diagram 9-20.)

"EVEN"

The tip again goes straight ahead. The small forward, (3), goes to the basket in his lane, and the quick guard, (2), reads the play. (See Diagram 9-21.)

SPECIALS

a. The tip is made to the small forward on the left, (3). At the same time, the big forward, (4), steps forward and screens the center's opponent. The center cuts for the basket and receives a lob pass from (3). (See Diagram 9-22.)

b. The tip is   straight ahead to the big forward, (4). The "quick" guard, (2), on the side makes a cut over the center, which impedes the movement of the defender on the safe guard, (1), who is cutting toward the basket. The small forward, (3), goes back on defense with the toss of the ball. The big forward with the ball, (4), may pass to guard, (1), who may be completely open, or pivot into the path of X^2 and hand the ball off to (2), who can go on his own. (See Diagram 9-23.)

c. A play similar to the one above may be run from a box formation. Both guards line up behind the jumper and the forwards, ahead. The center, (5), tips the ball ahead to the forward on his left,

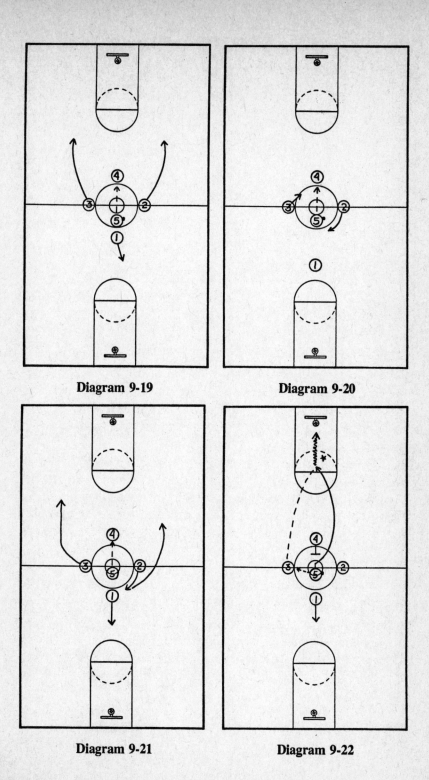

Diagram 9-19

Diagram 9-20

Diagram 9-21

Diagram 9-22

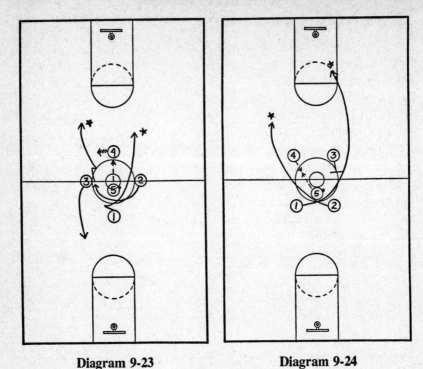

Diagram 9-23   **Diagram 9-24**

(4). The guards crisscross off the jumper, with the one on the ball side going first. The offside forward, (3), who did not receive the tip, steps forward and sets a definite screen on the defender of the guard moving his way, (1). (4) may pass to either of the guards. There is a good chance (1) will be open for a lay-up. (See Diagram 9-24.)

   d. At times, when the opposition appears to be gaining a definite advantage on us by getting every tip, we will use the "open spot" method on a tip-off and just attempt to secure the ball.

Last-second plays

   With just a few seconds left in a game, and a basket sorely needed to tie or win, a team should have a pre-planned and well-practiced play in their repertoire. Following are five such plays that may be used.

THE TOUCHDOWN PLAY

This play is run from the far end line against a man-to-man defense. It starts with all five offensive players in the back court. Three are at mid-court, one, (1), is the obvious inbounds passer, and the other, (2), is the obvious inbounds pass receiver. As (1) picks up the ball, (2) steps out of bounds. (The fact that the game was very close probably caused (1)'s defender, X^1, to play him very close.) (1) throws the ball cross court (out of bounds) to (2). Then, the middle man of the three mid-court men, (4), moves forward and sets a blind screen on (1)'s defender. (1) runs as fast as he can downcourt and receives a long pass from (2) for a basket. To keep the defensive men honest, both (3) and (5) move toward the backcourt baseline and call for the ball. (See Diagram 9-25.)

When playing against a team that switches a great deal on

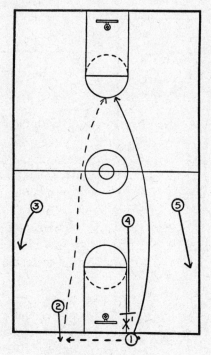

Diagram 9-25

defense, the switch option may be used. The play is run the same as before, but when it comes time for (4) to screen for (1), (4) sets the screen, calls out "switch," back pivots and runs downcourt to become the receiver of the "touchdown" pass from (2). (See Diagram 9-26.)

The step-in foul play

This play is again run from the backcourt baseline. It starts with (1) taking the ball out of bounds *after the opposition has scored*. (2) is at the free throw line, (4) is in the back court on the inbound passer's right side, (5) is at mid-court, and (3) is away from the play on the inbound passer's far left side at mid-court. After the score, (1) picks up the ball and steps out of bounds. As he does so, (2) moves up and blindscreens (1)'s defender on (1)'s right side. (1)

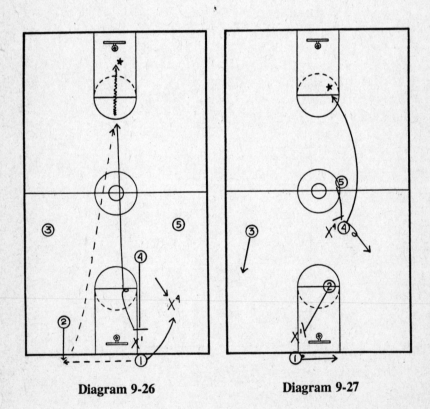

Diagram 9-26   **Diagram 9-27**

then runs to the right with the ball, attempting to run his defender into (2). If contact is made, (2) attempts to draw the step-in foul by falling down. At the same time, (5) sets a blind screen on (4)'s man. (4) cuts downcourt, looking for a pass from (1). If (4) is not open, (5) rolls to the sideline, takes a pass from (1), and calls time out. (See Diagram 9-27.) This play gives a team three chances in the last five seconds: (A) they may draw the step-in foul; (B) (4) may be open for the long pass; and (C) if nothing happens, the time-out is called with the ball almost at mid-court.

THE FRONT COURT WALL

This play is run in the front court to get that last-second basket. (1) is the inbound passer and (2) is at mid-court. The other three men, (3), (4), and (5), form a wall as shown in Diagram 9-28. As the play begins, (2) cuts to the back court, and the low man in the wall, (3), breaks up and toward the ball. It is hoped that his man will come with him. When this happens, (3) loops around the wall and receives a lob pass from (1). To clear their defensive men, (4) and (5) cut to the ball as soon as (3) loops around them. (See Diagram 9-29.) If (3)'s man does not come with him, (1) throws the ball to (3) and goes over the wall, looking for the lob from (3). (See Diagram 9-30.)

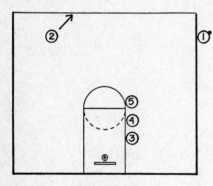

Diagram 9-28

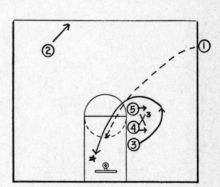

Diagram 9-29

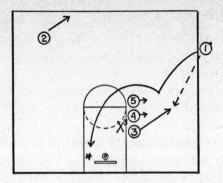

Diagram 9-30

THE PRESSURE STACK

This play takes advantage of a basic stack play, but under conditions where the defense is really denying the inbounds pass. Players (4) and (5), the two big men, line up in a stack free throw line high on the ball side. The ball is being taken out at mid-court by (1). X^4 and X^5 are trying to deny the inbounds pass as (4) steps out of the stack to the ball side. (1) quickly gets the ball to (4) on the sideline, and now X^5 is out of position to cover (5), who rolls for the basket and takes a lob pass from (4) for a lay-up. At the same time, (3) sets a blind screen for (2), who cuts for the basket on the far side of the court for a possible lob pass from (1) or (4). (See Diagram 9-31.) If neither is open, (3) rolls to the ball and takes the inbounds pass. (See Diagram 9-32.)

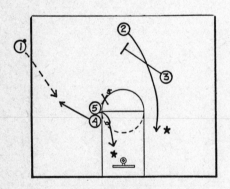

Diagram 9-31

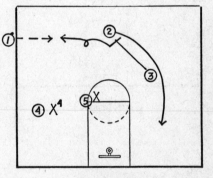

Diagram 9-32

THE MID-COURT LINE-UP

This formation is run with (1) again taking the ball out of bounds and players (2), (3), (4), and (5) lined up at mid-court on the ball side. (See Diagram 9-33.)

It starts when (5) goes over the top for a possible lob to the basket and (2) cuts to the back court. (See Diagram 9-34.)

The second phase is for (4) to screen for (3), who cuts straight to the ball. (4) then rolls to the basket for a possible lay-up shot. (See Diagram 9-35.)

These two phases must be run within a period of four seconds, and (1) must get the ball to the best possible option.

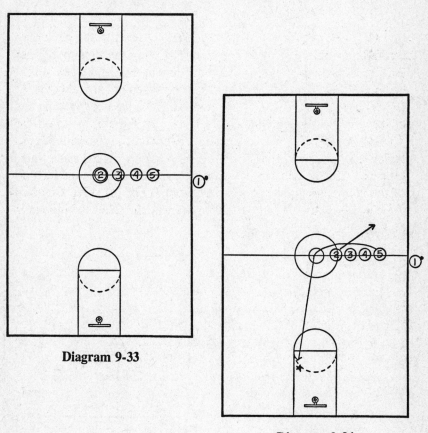

Diagram 9-33

Diagram 9-34

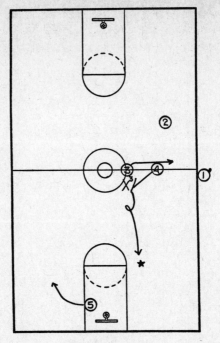

Diagram 9-35

THE FREE THROW PLAY

Fast breaking from a free throw

In this situation, the primary components are: the inside men must block out strong, the shooter must be cut off, a rebound must be acquired, a quick outlet must be made, and the three lanes must be filled. To do this, the two small men, (1) and (2), are stationed at mid-court, the two big men, (4) and (5), take the inside position, and the small forward, (3), is positioned to cut off the shooter. (See Diagram 9-36.)

When the rebound is obtained by (5), as in Diagram 9-37, the outlet man on his side, (2), wings out to take the pass. He then dribbles to the middle, and the cutoff man, (3), fills the ballside lane, that is, the side on which the outlet pass was made. (1) flies downcourt and (5) tries to get the ball to him. This happens occasionally when the opposition is attempting to cover (2) and stop the outlet pass.

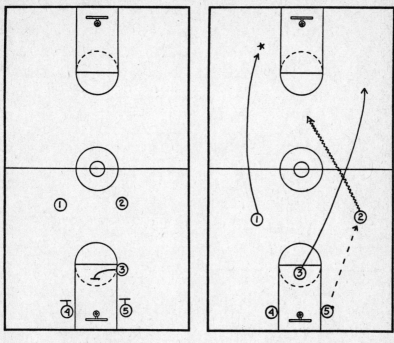

Diagram 9-36   Diagram 9-37

If (2) is not open when he wings out for the outlet pass, he comes back to the middle for it, and (3) hooks back. If (3) gets the pass from (5), he does one of two things—he may relay it on to the flying guard, (1), in the ballside corner (see Diagram 9-38), or he may dribble into the middle. (See Diagram 9-39.)

Defensing the fast break after a missed free throw

Many coaches will disagree with this method of defensing a missed free throw because they believe it is bad psychology to give your free throw shooter an assignment that takes place when he misses a free throw. But I feel that the first person to know when a free throw is missed is the shooter, and that this fact should be utilized.

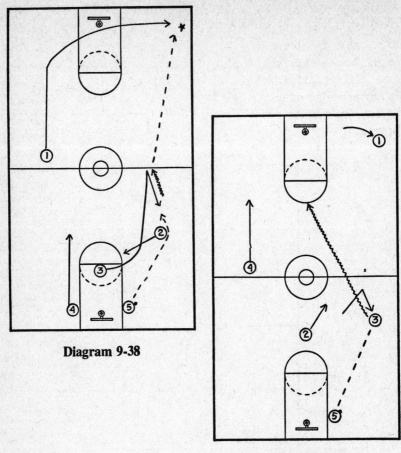

Diagram 9-38

Diagram 9-39

When using this method, you station two men in the second slots, two at mid-court, and, of course, your fifth man is the shooter. As soon as the shooter, (3), realizes he has missed and the ball has hit the rim, he fights his way to the middle of the lane. In most cases, he will be blocked out, but he must expect this and get around it. When the ball is obtained by the opposition, the mid-court man on that side, (2), must play for, and at least delay, the outlet pass. The offside mid-court man, (1), is responsible for protecting the basket. He is the safety man. The man in the second slot on the rebound side, (5), swarms the rebounder. Since the outlet pass is deterred by (2), the rebounder may pivot back inside. If so, he will be double-teamed by (3), who by this time has fought his way to the ball. The man in the second slot away from the rebound, (4), hustles to mid-court and prevents a pass to the middle. (See Diagram 9-40.)

This method, when used, gives a team the possibilities of: (A) intercepting the outlet, (B) double-teaming the rebounder, and (C) at least limiting the opposition's chances of organizing a fast break pattern.

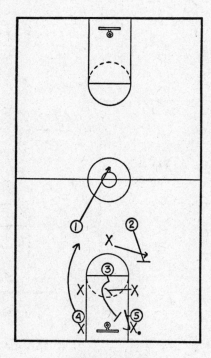

Diagram 9-40

10

STALLING

In recent years, the stall and control games have played an important part in the success of some of the great teams. They have been used, not only as a device to kill the clock at the end of games, but also as a change of pace early in the game. The intensity of today's pressure and help defenses has forced teams to play a cat and mouse type offensive game that takes advantage of defensive mistakes. Until these mistakes develop, the offense simply controls the ball and attempts to pull the defense out. Because of the success this type of game has enjoyed, it is certainly a trend to be aware of when planning your complete offensive strategy.

An ideal stall is one in which the offense is spread to disallow a lot of defensive help or double-teams, the ball is handled primarily by your best players, and it is kept away from your weak ball handlers and poor free throw shooters. Along with these factors, the threat of a score must be present at all times.

THE FOUR CORNER STALL

The stall that is most in vogue today is the four corner game. This stall puts your two big men, (4) and (5), one in each corner, and your three best ball handlers out front. The outside two front men, (2) and (3), are wide, and the middle man, (1), who is your top dribbling one-on-one man, dominates the ball. (See Diagram 10-1.)

From here, the following rules are observed by position:

The middle man is instructed that:

—He must be aware of being closely guarded and of making the penetration move in time. All the intricacies of this rule must be thoroughly understood by the entire team.

—If he passes the ball to one of the other front men, he should cut through, looking for a return pass, and if it isn't open, return to the front and fill an open side. (See (1) in Diagram 10-2.)

—If he dribbles through and is picked up by a big man's defender, to look for his corner playing teammate going baseline. (See Diagram 10-3.)

—Above all, he must take only very good percentage shots, and if they don't come, not to force a shot.

—He should pass to the big corner men if they break up.

The side men are instructed to:

—Stay wide and don't let their men help on the middle man. This is done by faking backdoor cuts and appearing to be open for a pass.

—Cut for the basket if the big man on their side breaks up and receives a pass from the middle man.

—Take the ball into the middle and go one-on-one if they receive a pass from the middle man.

—Get open if the middle man appears to be in trouble.

The big corner men are told to:

—Stay wide and keep your man busy, and if he is jamming from the offside, move up the sideline and call for the ball. (See (5) in Diagram 10-4.)

—Go baseline to the basket and look for the ball if the middle man penetrates on a dribble and your man helps.

—If the defender on the front man on your side of the court

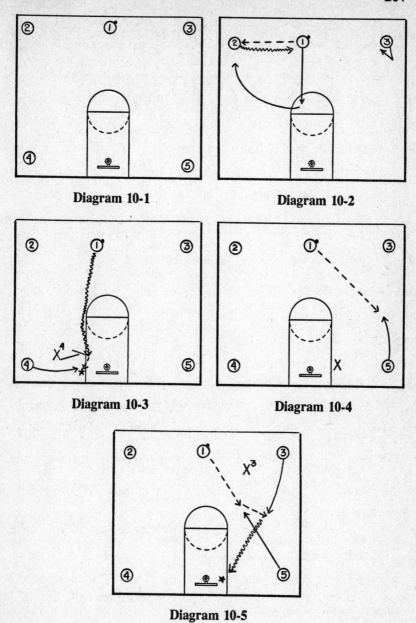

Diagram 10-1   Diagram 10-2

Diagram 10-3   Diagram 10-4

Diagram 10-5

sags off and helps on the middle man, allow your teammate to backdoor him by breaking up toward the middle man, taking a pass, and looking for your side man cutting for the basket. (See (5) in Diagram 10-5.)

THE FOUR MAN PASSING GAME STALL

The most basic rule of the passing game is to pass and go opposite. This in itself makes the passing game a good stall because it eliminates the double-team potential many teams attempt to capitalize on when the opposition is stalling. Another attribute of this formation is that the post man, who is not in the passing game movement, is stationed in the high post area and always provides a safety valve when the defense is really causing problems. The third big plus for using a four man passing game with a high post man for a stall is that the lane area is clear and breakaway situations can be taken advantage of. The following rules can be utilized:

The four basic movers

—There are four spots on the floor that, when filled, give us proper floor balance. They are two guard positions as wide as the lane and two forward positions foul line high and wide. (See Diagram 10-6.)

—After you pass the ball to a teammate, either screen opposite for the teammate nearest you, or cut straight for the basket and come out in the far corner. (See Diagram 10-7.)

—Try to pass the ball to men when they are moving toward you.

—If you come to the ball and cannot receive it, go through, or cut behind your man and go for the basket. Come out in the far corner.

—When you see an open man, pass to him. Don't hold the ball. Movement makes this offense work.

—If you are in the corner and make a pass, go to the baseline and then back toward the ball.

—If the initial guard-to-forward pass is pressured, the forwards may cross. (See Diagram 10-8.)

—When you are pressured and cannot get the ball to one of the basic movers, the post man will step out. When you pass to the post man and are in a guard position, you screen for the forward on your side, and the same thing happens on the offside. (See Diagram 10-9.)

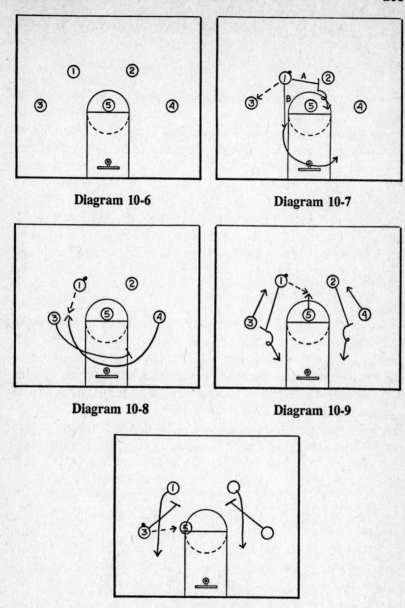

Diagram 10-6

Diagram 10-7

Diagram 10-8

Diagram 10-9

Diagram 10-10

—When you pass to the post from a forward position, you screen for the guard on your side, and the same thing happens on the off side. (See Diagram 10-10.)

—Don't waste your dribble. Use it to buy time or to make a breakaway play. When a teammate dribbles toward you, he wants you to clear out. You should clear to the far corner position. (See Diagram 10-11.)

—Try not to make the same move twice in a row when cutting off a screen. Come to the ball, cut through, go behind, and then go back and screen for a teammate.

—Never force the ball to a teammate cutting for the basket. If he is not 100 percent open, don't throw it.

—Move! Move! Move!

Post man's rules

—Step out when the basic movers need help. Come to meet the ball.

—After you receive the ball, look first for those being screened for, and secondly, for the rollers.

—If your opponent is sagging off to help on defense, step out more often.

—After you have given the ball to a mover, cut toward the basket and then back to the high post. (See Diagram 10-12.)

—Always give a teammate a passing target. Point your near elbow at your defender and hold your far arm out, keeping your body between the defender and the possible passing lane.

—Any time one of your teammates dribbles hard for the basket, your opponent will probably drop off to help. Roll to the basket, looking first for a pass, and second, to rebound a possible shot. (See Diagram 10-13.)

THE FIVE MAN PASSING GAME STALL

The formation that works best is to have a point man, (1), two wings, (2) and (3), and two wide corner men, (4) and (5). (See Diagram 10-14.)

The same rules as used by the basic movers in the four man passing rules prevail, with the following additions:

—When the point man makes his first pass to either wing, he will, in many cases, screen opposite for the offside wing. On this first pass, the offside wing, (3), should go with (1) and form a double screen for the offside corner man, (5). This is a very difficult play for X^5 to defend. If he fails to get over the double screen, (5)

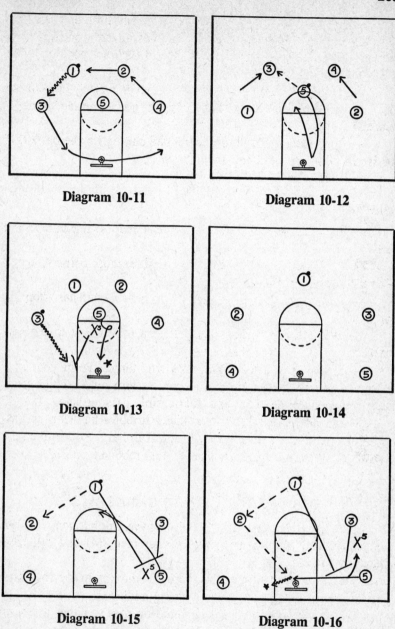

Diagram 10-11

Diagram 10-12

Diagram 10-13

Diagram 10-14

Diagram 10-15

Diagram 10-16

will have an easy cut to the ball. (See Diagram 10-15.) If X^5 fights over the double screen, (5) should go behind him and get a pass from (2) for a crossover lay-up shot. (See Diagram 10-16.)

—At any time, a player in the corner may break to the high post and take a pass. This keys his teammates to backdoor their overplaying defenders. (See Diagram 10-17.)

—Stay wide and don't jam the middle. When you cut through, clear to a corner, preferably the offside corner.

—The best area to attempt your one-on-one move is from the corner. If you beat your man from there, he probably will have no defensive help.

—One player will be designated to be the back man. If a shot is taken, or the ball is lost, he should be moving toward our defensive court. (See (1) in Diagram 10-18.)

THE HIGH POST STALL

This is a very simple stall that again uses the high post man as the safety valve man. The rules are as follows:

—Whenever the ball is passed to the post man, the guards exchange with the forwards on both sides. The forwards always backdoor first, and the guards are the screeners. (See Diagram 10-19.)

—When a guard-to-forward pass is made, both guards cut over the high post. The first guard, (1), goes over and through to the far corner, and the second guard, (2), goes through to the basket and then to the ballside corner. The offside forward, (4), comes out front, as does the forward with the ball on the dribble. (See Diagram 10-20.)

—When a pass is made from one guard position to the other (which is not a very good one to make), the passing guard, (1), exchanges with his forward, (3). (See Diagram 10-21.)

—The dribble chase is also used in this stall, and the player being chased always cuts first for the basket, and then to the far corner. (See Diagrams 10-22 and 10-23.)

—If the post man is being overplayed, (usually 3/4), a signal is given that tells him to backdoor for a lob pass. Very often, the signal will be a reverse dribble by a guard. (See Diagram 10-24.)

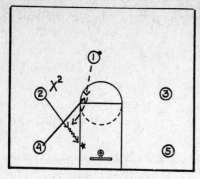

Diagram 10-17

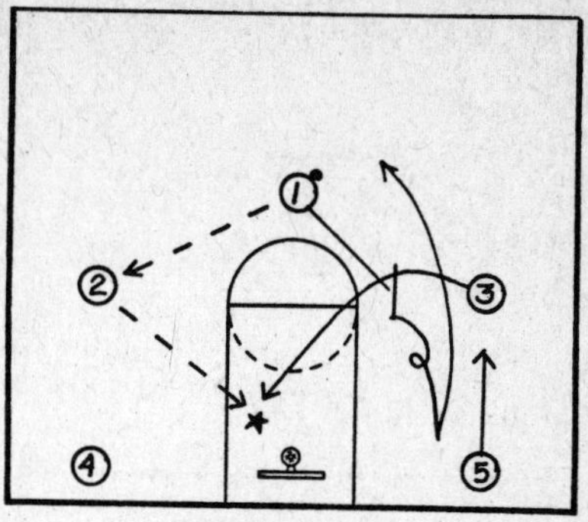

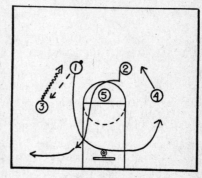

Diagram 10-18

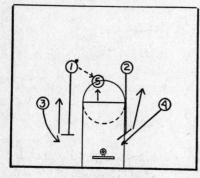

Diagram 10-19

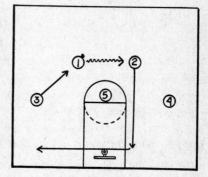

Diagram 10-20

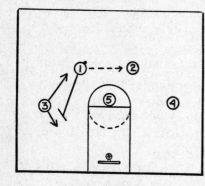

Diagram 10-21

Diagram 10-22

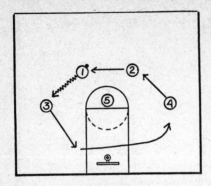
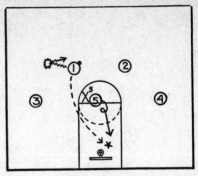

Diagram 10-23   Diagram 10-24

THE 3-2 STALL

This stall derives its name from its initial formation. One side of the court has a three man game and the other has a two man game.

The basic three man game

This is the side where most of the ball handling is done. It consists of the two guards and a forward, who is primarily a screener. One guard, (2), is stacked inside the forward, (3), and the other guard, (1), is out front with the ball. (2) comes out of the stack and receives the ball from (1). (1) then cuts to the basket for a possible return pass from (2). (See Diagram 10-25.) (2) then controls the ball until forward, (3), pinches in to stack with (1), who then gets open and the process is repeated. (See Diagram 10-26.) Anytime (1) or (2) are in trouble, forward, (3), steps up to the high post area to help. When a pass is made from the controlling guard, (1), to the forward coming high, (3), the other guard, (2), can very often backdoor for a lay-up shot. (See Diagram 10-27.)

The two man game

The two man game is very simple. They, (4) and (5) start in a high-low post set-up on the same side of the court. Whenever one of the guards in the three man game dribbles toward the two man game, (4) and (5) exchange positions, with the front man, (4), screening for the low man, (5), who comes out front. (See Diagrams 10-28 and 10-29.)

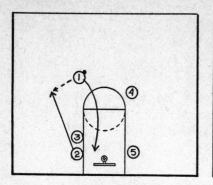

Diagram 10-25

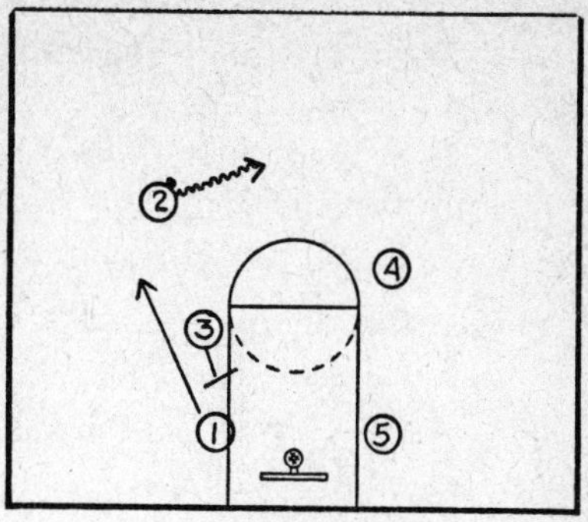

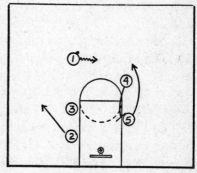

Diagram 10-26

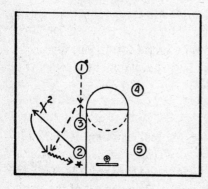

Diagram 10-27

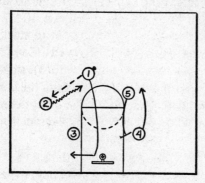

Diagram 10-28

Diagram 10-29

If the ball comes to the two man side, they may:

—Preferably get it back to the three man side, where the ball is being controlled.

—Work a screen and roll, two-on-two play. (See Diagram 10-30.)

—Post a weak defender.

—If (3)'s defender is causing trouble in the three man game, (5) may come over and screen for (3) when (4) receives the ball. This is a scoring option and allows for some changes in the three and two man games. (See Diagram 10-31.)

Interchangeable game

If you have five men of equal abilities, the three and two man games can be interchanged simply by allowing the player in the three man game who cuts down the middle to come out on either side. In this way, whichever side he comes out on becomes the three man game and the other becomes the two man game. (See Diagram 10-32 and Diagram 10-33.)

The same two options are available to the cutter, (4), after he throws the game to the two man side. He can keep the three man game on the same side by staying on that side. (See Diagram 10-34.) Or, (4) may change the sides of the two and three man games by cutting to the two man side. (See Diagram 10-35.)

This stall may also be used as a control type offense with great effectiveness.

STALLING VERSUS THE HALF COURT PRESSURE

One very important fact to remember when designing your basic offense is that it must be easily adaptable to meet defensive pressure tactics. That is to say, you must do one of two things—(1) have your basic offense and your offensive pressure game develop from the same formation or (2) have a pre-planned key that tells your players that they are being besieged by defensive pressure tactics. An example of this would be something as simple as telling your post man, who, in your offense, may play low, that he must break to the high post any time the guards are double-teamed.

At Eastern Montana College, we have always used a 2-1-2 offense featuring a high post man. This has made us very difficult to surprise with pressure because our offensive pressure game has utilized the same alignment. When attempting to stall, we have used the following rules from this formation any time a double-teaming, man-to-man or a half court zone press is used by the opposition.

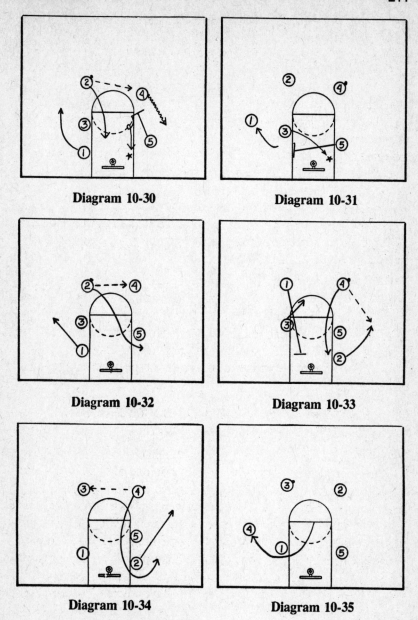

Diagram 10-30

Diagram 10-31

Diagram 10-32

Diagram 10-33

Diagram 10-34

Diagram 10-35

When a guard has the ball:

—The onside forward, (3), will always be as high as the head of the key and looking for a pass from his guard. (See Diagram 10-36.)

—The offside forward, (4), will be somewhere between the free throw line extended and the baseline. (See Diagram 10-36, above.)

—The offside guard, (2), will be as high as the ball.

—The post man, (5), will be on the side of the lane of the guard possessing the ball. He will always give you a passing target.

—The guards want to pass the ball to; first, the post, (5), if he is open; secondly, to their forward, (3); and if neither is open, to the other guard, (2). In some rare cases, they may throw a cross court lob pass to the offside forward, (4). (See Diagram 10-37.)

When the forwards have the ball:

—They first want to get the ball over their head and be prepared to throw a two hand overhead pass. This pass is best because it affords good protection of the ball while you are looking around, it can be thrown hard for distance, and it allows you to fake and change your mind at the last second.

—The forwards want to throw the ball first to the post man, (5), if he is open; second, to the offside guard, (2), who slides as low as the head of the key; third, back to the near guard, (1); and, on occasion, to the offside forward, (4), who may come across the lane. (See Diagram 10-38.)

When the post man has the ball:

—He looks first for the offside forward, (4), under the basket and, second, for the offside guard, (2). (See Diagram 10-39.)

—If in trouble, he will dribble toward mid-court and expect one of the guards to make a "V" and get open. (See Diagram 10-40.)

General rules

—Stay in the 2-1-2 shape and don't run around. This way the offense uses the entire court and makes double-teaming very difficult.

—Don't hold the ball; pass it to an open man.

—Use your dribble as a safety valve move.

—Don't be afraid to throw a cross court pass.

—All pass receivers must move to the ball.

—If they revert to a straight man-to-man, our guards will call out "Man!" and our pre-planned motion will be in order.

—Don't hurry. Jump balls are better than lost balls.

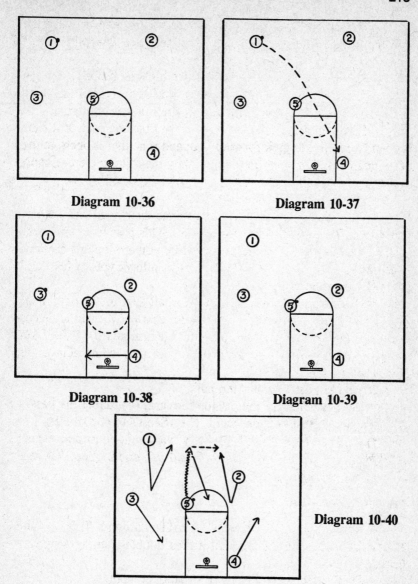

Diagram 10-36   Diagram 10-37

Diagram 10-38   Diagram 10-39

Diagram 10-40

—Know how much time is left on the clock, and shoot with six seconds to go.

—When you get the ball in the middle, a double-teaming defense is in trouble.

—Know how many time-outs we have remaining.

INDEX

Dan Dunn.